D0132414

# The
# Healing
# Journey

# The Healing Journey

## Overcoming the Crisis of Cancer

ALASTAIR J. CUNNINGHAM

KEY PORTER BOOKS

Copyright © 2000, 1992 by Alastair Cunningham

All rights reserved. No part of this work covered by the copyrights hereon may be reproduced or used in any form or by any means—graphic, electronic or mechanical, including photocopying, recording, taping or information storage and retrieval systems—without the prior written permission of the publisher, or in the case of photocopying or other reprographic copying, a license from the Canadian Copyright Licensing Agency.

**Canadian Cataloguing in Publication Data**

Cunningham, Alastair J. (Alastair James), 1940–
    The healing journey : overcoming the crisis of cancer

Rev.
Includes bibliographical references and index.
ISBN 1-55263-107-9

1. Cancer – Alternative treatment – Popular works. 2. Cancer – Treatment – Popular works. 3. Cancer – Psychological aspects – Popular work. 4. Mental healing. 5. Self–care, Health. I. Title.

RC262.C85 2000    616.99'406    C99–933085–3

The publisher gratefully acknowledges the support of the Canada Council for the Arts and the Ontario Arts Council for its publishing program.

We acknowledge the financial support of the Government of Canada through the Book Publishing Industry Development Program (BPIDP) for our publishing activities.

Key Porter Books Limited
Six Adelaide Street East
Tenth floor
Toronto, Ontario
Canada M5C 1H6

www.keyporter.com

Electronic formatting: Jean Lightfoot Peters
Design: Patricia Cavazzini

Distributed in the United States by Firefly Books

Printed and bound in Canada

05 06 07 08   7 6 5 4 3

# Contents

# Preface to the
# Second Edition

It is gratifying that *The Healing Journey* has done well enough to justify a second edition, and I thank the publishers at Key Porter for this opportunity. Many people, both cancer patients and health professionals, have written or called to say that the book has helped them, and I am delighted to have been a vehicle for this assistance. This second edition comes at a time when the spate of books on ways to help oneself, particularly against cancer, has become a flood, filling many rows of shelves in any large bookstore. The Internet, too, is now an extensive source of information (sometimes mis-information!) on this topic. On the whole, this trend is good, I think, since it demonstrates people's growing interest in using their own resources to maintain health, in addition to medical treatment. We need to be on guard, however, against the characteristics of floods: while they have great power, they pour heedlessly ahead over obstacles, without discriminating between what is worth preserving and what deserves to be swept away. So it is with popular accounts of mind-body healing. The more popular they are, the more reservations we may need to have about what they claim, since books become best sellers by telling people what they want to hear, and we all would like to believe that the power of the mind and spirit to heal is simply accessible and instantly potent. The reality is, of course, much more complex. *The Healing Journey* is unlikely to join the stacks at the entrance to bookstores, since it is an attempt, based on evidence and documented clinical experience, to provide a balanced account of what it is possible for the motivated patient to do to help herself or himself against cancer, and the kinds of effort this requires. This is, in brief, much more than biomedicine currently believes, but less than many of the more messianic accounts imply. Wonderful healing transformations are possible for at least some individuals, but they require great effort and dedication.

In the scientific arena, "Psycho-oncology," meaning the study of the relationship between mind and cancer, has become an accepted specialty, as a branch of the larger field known as Health Psychology or Behavioral Medicine. Things move slowly in this kind of research, much to the exasperation of many people battling cancer. For example, it can take five years or more to test the impact of a psychological therapy on the quality or length of life of people with cancer. And such research is difficult and underfunded—most researchers opt for easier projects, like surveying the attitudes of cancer patients towards their disease or aspects of their health care. However, progress has been made since 1992. In this new edition I will describe (in Chapter 5) some of the recent research on whether group psychological therapy can prolong average survival for people with metastatic cancer, as well as our own studies on the kinds of attitudes and behaviors that correlate with living longer.

My own life since the first edition? I feel profoundly grateful to be still alive and well, after some sixty years of life, when it could have ended, because of cancer, in my late forties. It seems clearer than ever to me that the main purpose of one's life is to try to understand who and what we are (this includes a wide range of both personal and professional endeavors in many fields), and then to use this understanding to help others. For me, the personal work is improving self-understanding through psychological reflection and through spiritual practices and reading; the professional work is devising ever more comprehensive courses for motivated patients, and attempting to document, through close observation of what these people say and do, just what kinds of change prolong life. As this understanding improves, it is a privilege to have the chance to pass it on to interested readers.

*Toronto, November 1999*

# Preface to the
# First Edition

A diagnosis of cancer is one of the greatest challenges any of us will ever have to face. It comes to about a million people each year in the United States and Canada. More than a quarter of us in Western countries will be confronted with it at some time in our lives. The unwelcome news provokes shock, disbelief, fear, and often anger and depression. Immediately, we want to know: "Why did this happen to me? What can modern medicine do to eliminate this threat to my life?" If the disease has been found at an "early" stage—that is, before it has obviously spread to sites away from its primary location (metastasized)—a tumor can often be removed with a reasonable chance that it will not return and additional tumors will not appear. In about half of all cases, however, medical treatment does not "cure," and the person eventually dies of the disease.

Most people who are diagnosed as having cancer sensibly view medical treatment as their first line of defense. However, more and more people are asking whether there are steps they can take to help themselves, both to cope better with the great stress a life-threatening illness causes and to make long-term survival, and perhaps cure, more probable. This question has generated strong opinions both for and against. On the "conservative" side, the science of biomedicine sees cancer as a collection of aberrant cells that can be removed or killed only by some external treatment. On what might be called the "radical" or "New Age" side, a confusing array of popular books and articles exists, many of them claiming that cancer can be overcome with simple "alternative" procedures, such as special diets or psychological tricks. Not surprisingly, the two sides in this debate do not communicate well with each other. The person with cancer is unfortunately caught in the middle, wanting desperately to get well, wondering if medical treatment will be enough, and not knowing which, if any, to believe among the various claims made about alternative, self-help types of treatment.

This book is intended to provide a reasoned account of what we can do to help ourselves against cancer, a middle way between the extreme conservatism of modern Western medicine and the unfounded radicalism of a lot of New Age thinking. I am a scientist, which may put some readers on the defensive, while reassuring others. However, I have worked therapeutically with hundreds of cancer patients, and have had cancer myself; I try to take an open-minded attitude to unconventional methods of health care, and have personally used many of them. *The Healing Journey* is my attempt to help you make rational decisions about responsible and effective self-help against cancer.

## Who is this book for?

I had two main groups of people in mind while writing this book. The first were cancer patients and their families. In particular, the book is aimed at the *thoughtful* patient, the person who wants to consider the evidence and make his or her own decisions about what can usefully be done to aid in the struggle to stay well. It will not appeal to someone who simply wants to adopt a scheme of self-treatment that is advocated strongly but not supported by any proof or rationale for its effectiveness; there is, unfortunately, a great deal of this sort of advice on the market. The book should also help family members and friends of patients who want to be informed about possible additional modes of care for their loved ones.

The second main group for whom this book is written includes the many physicians, psychologists, social workers, nurses, pastoral-care counselors, members of other helping professions, and laypersons who are interested in trying to help people with cancer or other chronic diseases. For those members of this group who are skeptical about nonmedical interventions, I hope this book demonstrates that many of the things patients can do to help themselves make good sense. For those who are already persuaded of this, I hope it provides a touchstone against which to evaluate your own ideas.

Will this book be useful to people with problems other than cancer? I think so, although my own clinical experience is largely with cancer patients and their families. Rational self-help is mainly about strengthening the body's defenses against disorder by promoting a balance between all parts of oneself and the environment. These principles apply to all of us, whether or not we have a "disease"; indeed, most of us could improve this balance, and enjoy better health than we usually do.

## What potential do we have to help ourselves?

Most people have a great deal of potential to help themselves. We see this ability at work in such activities as establishing a home, training for a career, and managing personal finances. Yet the idea that we can do anything significant when faced with serious disease, except take medical treatment, is largely viewed as unconventional in Western society Many have the will to help themselves, even the conviction that it is possible to do so, but are unsure what to do about it, beyond adopting a few obvious healthy behaviors. This book is written for such individuals; it attempts to provide a rationale for organizing efforts at self-help.

What can we reasonably expect from self-help? First, we can

expect to improve the *quality* of our lives. For most cancer patients, most of the time, the worst pain is not physical, but emotional: fear of degeneration and death, of leaving loved ones, of plans and hopes not being fulfilled. Such techniques as deep relaxation, mental imaging, and meditation, along with the sense of control that comes from learning them, can lift depression and anxiety and create a new sense of meaning in life, however long or short that life may be. Second, there is growing evidence, which we will discuss later, that mental self-help may favorably affect the progress of disease. Scientific data now exist showing that psychological support or therapy may prolong the survival of people with advanced cancer, and it is reasonable to suggest that mental change may render recurrence of the disease less likely in people whose primary tumors have been removed. Even advanced cancers will occasionally (very rarely) disappear in the absence of any significant medical treatment, a phenomenon known as "spontaneous" remission. It must be acknowledged at the outset, however, that there are limits to what we can do, and that our knowledge about how to mobilize our internal resources is still rudimentary. Nevertheless, a great deal of useful information is already available.

### What does this book cover?

I should say at the outset what this book is not. First, it is not a collection of stories about people who have had remarkable recoveries from advanced disease. I have known such people, and understand that reading about them can be very reassuring, but will leave the reader to consult the numerous accounts in the popular literature (some of the better ones are listed in "Further Reading"). Second, it is not primarily intended as a workbook. (A practical guide, *Helping Yourself*, has been published as a workbook and two audiotapes by the Canadian Cancer Society; it can be obtained from them.) The task this book undertakes is to survey the field of self-help approaches, and help you plan your own "healing journey." Once you have a plan, you will be able to tap your community's resources, including other books, in a more efficient way.

My main aim here has been to cover a wide range of approaches to healing, from the very concrete methods of modern medicine to the exciting, although still largely unproven idea that our minds may influence cancer, and on to some of the difficult but important existential questions: "Is there some meaning to my disease, and to my life? Is there something more to me than just body and mind, and, if so, how can I become connected to this spiritual dimension?" Most books on helping ourselves against cancer focus on one part of this spectrum, usually either the medical or the psychological approaches. The attempt here has been to survey the whole field, and to do it from a rational perspective, in a spirit of enquiry, rather than by dogmatic assertion. The spiritual dimension, in particular, is usually avoided or dealt with in a cursory fashion in books about self-help, and in counseling generally, but it is my experience that it is immensely important to many people with life-threatening diseases, and that useful insights can be reached in an open-minded, nondogmatic way.

## What sources of knowledge will we draw on?

If you are thinking of embarking on a journey, it may help to know something about your guide's credentials and sources of information. I draw on three main kinds of experience in this book: my scientific training and reading of the scientific literature, clinical practice, and my own struggles with cancer and with techniques for personal understanding and growth.

My original training was in veterinary medicine and general biology, after which I took a Ph.D. in cell biology and did research for nearly twenty years in immunology at various institutions, most recently at the Ontario Cancer Institute, Canada's largest cancer treatment and research facility. From about 1980 my work changed, while I was doing a second doctorate in clinical psychology, to the investigation of the beneficial effects of counseling and coping-skills training for cancer patients. My main professional interest in recent years has been understanding how the mind may affect the body and influence health. This background as an investigator has taught me that, although science can be very conservative at times, the habits of critical thought and experiment provide a much-needed safeguard against the tendency we all have to believe what we want to believe, whether or not it is supported by evidence.

The second area we will be drawing on is my clinical experience working with cancer patients, together with the published experience of many other people. Since 1982, I have developed and directed a series of courses at the Ontario Cancer Institute called the Cancer Coping Skills Training Program, offering support to groups of cancer patients and their families, and teaching specific methods of coping with and opposing the disease. There are now about fifteen of us—psychologists, social workers, and other counselors—conducting the program, which has become one of the largest of its kind in North America. The beneficial effects of the program on the quality of life of hundreds of patients have been extensively documented, and we are currently beginning to test the effect of support and self-help training on lifespan.

The third source of information behind this book is more personal knowledge. I have explored many ways of trying to understand myself, the most important being long-term psychoanalytic psychotherapy and the practice of integral yoga. I find that grappling with my own problems and reasons for existence—an ongoing process—helps very much in understanding and empathizing with others; in fact, it is an essential prerequisite for this work. A few years ago I was diagnosed as having bowel cancer, and I responded by greatly increasing the intensity of my own search for "connectedness" with all aspects of my being—physical, psychological, social, and spiritual. However, I do not claim to be a "miraculous survivor"; the surgery and chemotherapy I received could account for my current good health, although the practice of self-help techniques was of enormous value in coping with the disease, and it may well have improved my chances of survival.

The sum of this experience provides the foundation for this book. Since it is intended for the layperson, explanations will be nontechnical and as simple as I can make them. I have elected not to interrupt the text with a lot of references; thus it is not a scholarly work. However, some major sources are acknowledged, and a list of additional reading is provided. You will find that it also differs from most popular books in that I take care to acknowledge the origin of information behind statements made; I cite the scientific evidence and the consensus of clinical opinion, where these exist, and alert the reader when I venture into areas of private experience.

### What will we conclude?

At the end of this guidebook to "the healing journey," we will find that, if a person is willing to make an effort to try new patterns of behavior and thought, then the experience of having cancer or other chronic disease may become very different from our usual conception of it as unmitigated disaster. At the very least, quality of life—that is, mood, sense of hope and control, and interactions with other people—can, in most cases, be greatly improved. It increasingly seems probable, although research evidence is not conclusive as yet, that life can be longer as well as better. The most favorable outcome of adopting a self-help approach to illness is that the experience of disease itself comes to have meaning, to be part of a continuum of meaningful events in life; by studying and struggling with illness the individual learns and evolves. This view may seem absurd to the newly diagnosed patient who just wants someone or something to take away his or her disease; however, many of our patients have reached this level of understanding. At the end of the book, the reader will see that what we have done is simply to rediscover ancient wisdom—the doctrine of harmony and wholeness—and to cast it in modern terms. It is a wisdom that has been almost forgotten in our materialistic and technological world.

*1992*

# Acknowledgments
# to the First Edition

This book is a product of my own continuing journey toward healing—my attempt to understand why we are here, and the meaning of events, such as disease, that happen to us during our lives. Many people have helped me along the way, and so have indirectly contributed to the text. My parents, first of all, with their dedication to learning; many fine teachers at school; and, later, scientific colleagues and mentors. More recently, psychological teachers and therapists have helped me greatly to enlarge my limited view of reality and to understand how we contribute to its construction. I have been lucky enough to have a highly supportive and nurturing family environment, and have learned a great deal from my wife, Margaret, and two children, John and Anne.

Colleagues at our Cancer Coping Skills program and at the Ontario Cancer Institute have given much helpful advice and support during the preparation of this book; the following people kindly read part or all of the manuscript: Tom Thomson; Brydon Gombay; Dick Hasselback, M.D.; David Warr, M.D.; Claire Edmonds; Gwen Jenkins; Herbert Pollack, C. Psych.; Anne Armstrong-Gibson; Margaret Cunningham; and Swami Radha Krishnananda. My secretary, Amy Lee, has been unfailingly helpful and reliable, and our program coordinator, Gwen Jenkins, a dedicated and valued colleague. To all of these people I extend my thanks; I can repay the debt only by trying to be equally helpful to others.

There are two groups I must mention more specifically. The first is Swami Sivananda Radha and her students at Yasodhara Ashram, British Columbia, and elsewhere. I have been extremely fortunate to encounter such a sincere community dedicated to the spiritual search, and have been able to orient my life more authentically as a result of their example. The second group includes the many hundreds of cancer patients and their family members who have attended our programs over the past ten years. It has been a great privilege to know many of these people at a critical point in their lives: my love and respect extend to all of them, whatever they have been able to do. I hope that, through the medium of this book, their struggles with cancer have been transmuted into something that may help many others.

## Part One

# The Onset
# of Cancer

# 1 | "IT'S CANCER! What Do I Do Now?"

In this brief chapter we will describe some of the feelings and reactions people often have to a diagnosis of cancer; you may have experienced many of them yourself. I then outline the path we will follow in considering how you can help yourself.

## Reactions to the Diagnosis

Typically, the first reaction to a diagnosis of cancer is shock, incredulity: "This can't be happening to me. Cancer is something other people get!" The shock may induce an emotional numbness, which protects us for a while from the full impact of what the diagnosis means. The fact that the person communicating the bad news, usually a doctor, may be quite matter-of-fact about it, having had to play this role fairly often, contributes to our sense of the unreality of the situation. However, within a space of time that varies, according to the person, from a few seconds to several days or more, the true nature of the situation "strikes home"—for once, the trite phrase is accurate; it can really feel like being struck at our very core. Then we may experience great fear, even terror. We may be overwhelmed with sadness or depression; we may be angry, and understandably so, since our plans for life have been grossly interfered with. Or there may be other, unexpected reactions; some people report feeling relief—"Thank goodness! Now I can get out of this marriage/job/life situation." We may shun thoughts like these because we are "not supposed" to think this way.

As the mind begins to absorb the blow, it looks for ways to relieve the emotional pain. We want desperately to minimize the threat to life posed by the diagnosis; thus, many people with, say, a primary cancer of the breast cling to the belief that surgery will remove all risk, ignoring the possibility of recurrence. We label this kind of mental defense "denial," meaning that the reality of a situation is not acknowledged. Sometimes denial takes irrational forms: some people convince themselves that their X-rays have been mixed up with someone else's, or that other test results are somehow invalid. Anger can be a way of venting some of the strong emotion, and it is common for patients to be unreasonably angry at health care personnel, who may unwittingly provide a focus for this pent-up feeling.

As the days pass, extreme sadness mixed with apprehension commonly sets in. Where once we saw ourselves as healthy, we suddenly seem vulnerable and ill, and we may withdraw from normal social or sexual activity. We wonder what is going to happen to us: will we die, be taken away from our loved ones, perhaps suffer great pain? Some people quickly mobilize a fighting spirit: "No little cancer cells are going to get me!" Others are more pessimistic. For me, after the fear, the worst thoughts were imagining my family having to manage without me. Chronic anxiety and depression often develop. It may seem that nothing is worthwhile any more, that we are diminished, worthless, no longer fully human.

## Reactions of family members

The people close to someone diagnosed as having cancer will typically experience a range of strong emotions also. There is usually shock and dismay, mixed with sympathy for the affected person. Family and friends may feel helpless, even bewildered, at what is happening, and may withdraw emotionally from the patient because they don't know what to say, or because it is too painful to contemplate losing a loved one. Other emotions that are common although not usually disclosed are anger, because one's plans are disrupted, or guilt from feeling that somehow one may have contributed to the situation, or because it seems impossible to do enough to help, or even for being well while a loved one is sick.

## What Should I Do With These Reactions?

First, it is essential to realize that whatever you feel and think is legitimate. There are reasons for how we respond to life crises, reasons rooted in our past. Second, it is important to be aware that we all tend, to varying extents, to *repress* these feelings, that is, to avoid experiencing them, because they are so uncomfortable. It is vital that we acknowledge to ourselves what we really feel—if we feel like crying, to cry; if we want to roar with rage, to do so, at an appropriate time. If the emotions are denied rather than acknowledged, they don't go away, but may manifest as chronic anxiety or depression, or as discomfort when we interact with others. However, if the fear is very great it is wise to let it into our awareness a little bit at a time, or it may seem overwhelming.

The next step is to share with others what we are feeling. In our counseling groups, we see all the time the great value of honest sharing between people with cancer; this kind of discussion can feel like letting a load drop from one's shoulders as the tension and pressure dissolve, at least for a time. Talking to a skilled counselor can also be extremely valuable; doing so is not a sign of weakness, as some seem to assume, but is a sensible, self-caring tactic. We may be inhibited from expressing our pain by a sense that we have to protect others from it; this is misguided self-sacrifice, and in fact, family members will usually appreciate being taken into your confidence. Similarly, don't allow others to constantly smooth over or minimize what's going on—"You're going to be all right; they have drugs that can cure you" or "You look great; we'll beat this thing." There are times when such assurance is helpful, but if we feel really hopeless, we need others to respect that feeling and not to alleviate their own anxiety at our expense.

Some spouses, particularly husbands, will withdraw emotionally from an affected partner; you, the patient, may have to tell them that you need support and genuine communication. When our lives are threatened, we need to know we are still loved, that we still matter and won't be abandoned. More distantly related family and friends will have their own coping styles, and, again, you will have to decide which individuals you find it helpful to talk honestly to and which ones to avoid when you are feeling low. A man in one of our groups is very forthright about this; he has told friends and family that he doesn't want to discuss his cancer with them until they are able to be clear what they themselves really feel about it. Colleagues at work may avoid the subject and distance themselves from you. Unfortunately, the person with cancer has to do a lot of educating of others if he or she wants the best support.

Ultimately, most people with cancer settle into a mental state in which they try not to think about it too much, although there are still bad times, particularly at night. This is sometimes called "getting on with your life," and, of course, there is a lot of appeal to it: nobody wants to worry all the time. It is the culturally sanctioned norm, the kind of adjustment that professionals generally regard as the best possible for their patients. But we must realize that, if we have a life-threatening disease, that fact is a very important part of our life. By denying the reality of such a threat, we are staying in a passive mode, failing to respond in a fully human way, which is something most of us would not advocate in the face of any other kind of threat to life or well-being. Our challenge will be to find a way of adjusting to cancer that, without making us anxious, helps us to cope with and even master the threat.

### How do I decide on a course of action?

This book takes you through a range of possible ways of responding to cancer. Its first task will be to explain what cancer is and how the body tries to control it (Chapter 2). This subject is unavoidably somewhat technical, since it involves scientific work in biology, although I have tried to write it for the nonspecialist. I then outline Western medicine's approach to cancer, in Chapter 3. It would be foolish not to think first of medicine in our treatment plan; modern diagnostic techniques are very sophisticated and can usually tell us what we are up against. Treatment is sometimes effective, sometimes not, as I will discuss. Then, in Chapter 4, we look at alternative or unorthodox remedies, a route many people want to explore. Here I have tried not to make judgments but to supply the tools to do your own critical appraisal of these methods.

Colleagues who read this book in manuscript told me that Chapters 2, 3, and 4 would be rather difficult, and often depressing, for most lay readers. I have revised them, but the concepts and approaches are those of modern science and medicine and will inevitably seem to many readers rather dry and impersonal compared with the later chapters of the book. Where these chapters are depressing, it is because the facts about cancer and its treatment are often so. However, these sections form a kind of biomedical foundation on which we can build; readers whose interests are primarily in the mental and intuitive domain can skip directly to Chapter 5 or 6.

The main body of the book is about "healing from within," or making changes in our mental attitudes and behaviors that may promote healing. Chapter 5 summarizes the scientific evidence for an influence of mind on cancer. In this edition I have added a discussion of new results from the last few years. In Chapter 6, we develop a theory to explain how and why our minds affect healing, a possibility that has been largely neglected by modern medicine. Then, in Chapters 7 to 10, we will look at the practical strategies that we can learn to use to assist our healing. This part of the book you will probably find much more "up-beat" or positive in tone, although as a scientist I have to point out that we are relying here on a different kind of evidence: not scientific experiments, but the accumulated experience of many people, including some cancer patients, who have devoted their energies to self-understanding and healing.

We will end on a very positive note, with an idea that I alluded to in the Preface, that cancer, like everything else in our lives, has meaning. Some readers will already understand this; to others it may seem absurd, even offensive. I can only say that this is what the healing journey is ultimately about—discovering that life, and everything that happens within it, has meaning in a larger context. If you are willing to be open to this possibility and to undertake the journey, you can experience its truth for yourself.

# 2 The Biology of Cancer

Before examining in detail how we can help ourselves, we need to have some background about what cancer is and how our bodies react against it. This chapter will provide some basic facts on the biology of the disease and its incidence and medical classification, and will outline what is known about the body's defense mechanisms.

## What is cancer?

Cancer is a group of more than one hundred diseases whose common characteristic is the exaggerated growth of abnormal cells. Many kinds of cells can be affected. In all of them the first steps toward development of a "tumor," or abnormal mass of cells, are changes (mutations) in the genes, that is in the genetic material or DNA in the nucleus of the cell. Research over the last few years has identified particular "oncogenes" or cancer genes; changes in these genes set a cell on the path toward becoming cancerous. It is believed that at least two, and often as many as five or six or more of these changes must take place in a cell before it is fully "malignant" or cancer-producing. These alterations are then passed on to the daughter cells as cell division occurs. Cells can become abnormal or "premalignant" in tissues that are subject to continual irritation, but then revert to normal appearance and behavior after a time once the irritation stops. A good example of this process is the series of changes that take place in the bronchial lining of a smoker's lungs: more and more cells are changed with time, becoming increasingly likely to produce fully malignant offspring. When smoking stops, the population of cells slowly reverts to normal again. Cancer biologists speak of the first genetic event as "initiation" and of subsequent changes as "promotion" of the cancerous transformation in the cell. Thus, the beginning of a cancer is not a single, cataclysmic event, but a gradual progression. There is typically a latent period of some years between the first abnormal changes and visible tumor growth.

The main property of cells we might call "fully malignant" is that, unlike normal cells, which divide only a limited number of times, they keep on dividing, and are not adequately controlled by the hormones and other molecules that limit the multiplication of normal cells. The average rate of division will affect the speed at which a tumor develops; it may be fast—once every few days—although it is usually much slower—once a month or less. Imagine that all the cells of a tumor are dividing once a week; there will be two by the second week, four by the third, eight by the fourth, and so on. (This progression is illustrated in Figure 1.) If you continue the calculation, you will see that we arrive at around one thousand million cells by the thirtieth week, an accumulation that may form a visible tumor about one centimeter in diameter and one gram in weight. If this rate of division continues for another ten weeks, the mass will reach one kilogram, usually enough to kill a person. Tumors don't grow quite as steadily as this, but the example indicates how a dangerous cancer can develop quickly from a single microscopic cell.

As this malignant family of cells grows, some of its members change still further. For example, new variants may appear that grow faster, or are more resistant to drugs, and outgrow their less

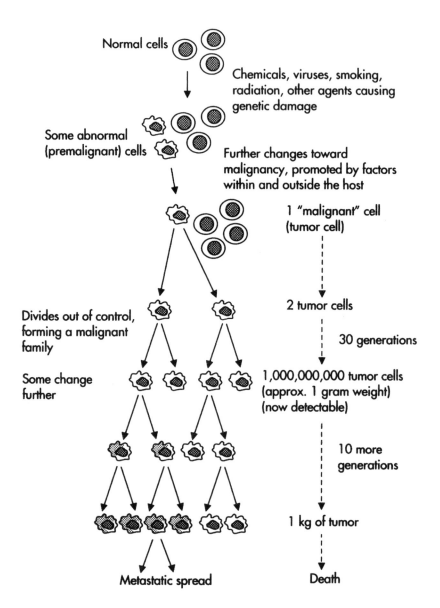

Normal cells

Chemicals, viruses, smoking, radiation, other agents causing genetic damage

Some abnormal (premalignant) cells

Further changes toward malignancy, promoted by factors within and outside the host

1 "malignant" cell (tumor cell)

2 tumor cells

Divides out of control, forming a malignant family

30 generations

Some change further

1,000,000,000 tumor cells (approx. 1 gram weight) (now detectable)

10 more generations

1 kg of tumor

Metastatic spread

Death

Figure 1
*Stages in the gradual development of cancer.*

dangerous brethren. Under the microscope, these later cells are often large, with irregular outlines, and bear little resemblance to the cells of the tissue of origin. Their most dangerous property is not so much their unrestrained multiplication at one site as the potential they have to detach from the original tumor and spread around the body to form new foci of growth, a process called metastasis (from the Greek for "change in place"). We classify as "benign" tumors those that grow but do not spread; they can usually be removed completely. Malignant tumors invade the surrounding tissues and tend to metastasize, making their complete removal difficult or impossible.

## What causes cancer?

What, then, is the cause of cancer? Should we refer to these cellular mutations as the ultimate cause, or does something else trigger them? While it is now known that some people (a small minority) inherit genes that make them prone to acquiring cancer later in life (there are at least two such genes for breast cancer, for example, affecting about 5 percent of women), most of the factors provoking cancer seem to come from the environment around cells, and often ultimately from outside the body. Different factors, acting at different levels, influence the chance that we will get the disease, as Figure 2 shows. Various environmental conditions affect personal behaviors, which in turn may increase the likelihood of cellular mutations. As these mutations increase in frequency, the probability rises that a number will occur within the same cell in a way that produces a cancer. The mind, as we will see later, plays a role both by controlling behavior and by directly affecting the internal "environment" in the body.

Experts consider that, in Western society, as many as 85 percent of all cancers are related to environmental influences, particularly lifestyle habits, and are thus preventable! The two major culprits are diet and smoking. The evidence for diet is indirect. The incidence rate of some cancers varies greatly from one part of the

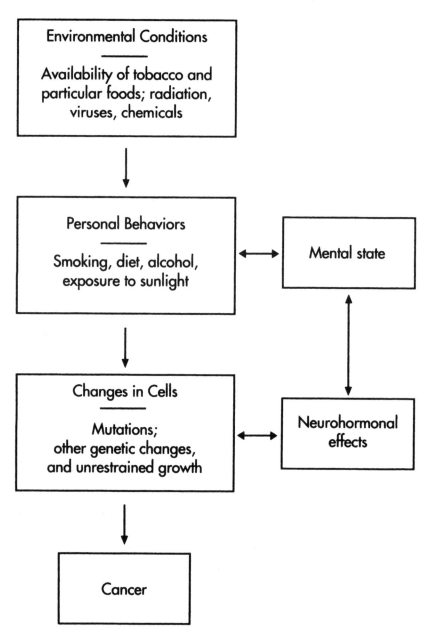

Figure 2

*Some of the many factors, both from within the individual and from without, that may influence the development of cancer.*

world to another. The differences are not genetic, since when people move from one country to another, their risk of getting these cancers gradually changes to become the same as experienced by the native population of the new country. For example, cancer of the breast is, or has been, relatively rare among Japanese living in Japan, but approaches the U.S. level of incidence in Japanese who have moved to the United States. For stomach cancer among the Japanese, the reverse is true: risk is high while they live in Japan and low after they move to the United States. The most likely explanation, supported by other indirect evidence, is diet.

It is estimated that about 35 percent of all cancers are attributable to diet. High levels of dietary fat may increase the risk of cancer of the colon, breast, and uterus, and low dietary fiber may increase susceptibility to colon cancer, although it is important to note that the evidence is not yet conclusive: the experts still disagree among themselves. The official recommendation at present for reducing risk is to avoid overeating, limit fat intake, and consume a lot of fruit and vegetables. (More details can be obtained from such sources as the local branch of your national cancer society. As I discuss in Chapter 4, there is no good published evidence for the idea that various unconventional diets or food additives such as vitamins can prevent cancer, much less cure it.)

The picture is clearer for smoking. The risk of lung cancer is increased about ten times by long-term smoking of ten cigarettes a day—and up to sixty times by smoking forty a day! Cigar and pipe smoking carries lower risks. The incidence of lung cancer among women is rising dramatically, as young women take up smoking. Smoking is estimated to account for about 30 percent of all cancers, and it contributes to many other conditions, such as heart disease, emphysema, and bronchitis.

Other lifestyle-related contributors to the high rates of cancer in our society are heavy consumption of alcohol (cancers of the mouth, esophagus, larynx, and liver), prolonged exposure to sunlight (skin cancer, including melanoma), and multiple sexual partners early in life (cancer of the cervix). Certain environmental contaminants, such as asbestos or industrial chemicals in some areas, may promote cancer; some drugs, particularly those used to treat cancers or to prevent rejection of transplanted organs, may themselves cause tumors. Viruses are a prominent cause of cancer in animals, but are known to be involved in only a few kinds of human cancer: a particular kind of lymphatic cancer found in Africa, a primary liver cancer, a type of leukemia (affecting white blood cells), and cancer of the cervix. Most human cancers are not infectious and are not transmitted from one person to another.

My intention here is not to provide a comprehensive summary of what is known about factors promoting cancer (for more details you can consult some of the excellent popular accounts, such as *Understanding Cancer* by John Laszlo)[1], but to convey one important fact about cancer: it is not caused by a single isolated, unavoidable "act of God," but is a gradual process, to which environmental conditions, our personal behavior, and cellular genetic changes all contribute. Even after malignant cells appear, some control of their growth is possible. People tend to think of getting cancer as being like "catching" an infectious disease; by accident, we encounter a virus or bacterium and are then inevitably struck by the disease. That, too, is an oversimplification, since the onset of infectious disease also depends greatly on host factors. For cancer, even more than for infections, the final disease is the product of various influences acting over a long time. There is hope that we can interrupt this process at a number of points.

### Types, stages, and incidence of cancer

Cancers are classified by the organ or tissue in which they first appear, by the microscopic appearance of the cells, and by their behavior, that is, the extent to which they tend to spread in a malignant fashion. The two main categories of malignant tumor are "carcinomas," which come from epithelial tissue (the cells covering most of the surface of the body), and "sarcomas," which develop from connective tissue (for example, bone, blood, and cartilage). There are many subcategories; for example, there are two main kinds of carcinomas. Squamous-cell carcinomas show some features of the flattened-out cells covering the skin, mouth cavity, esophagus, anus, and outer cervix; adenocarcinomas are carcinomas in which the cells are arranged in the form of glands. Two types of sarcomas are leukemias, or malignancies of the blood-forming organs, and "lymphomas," tumors of the lymph glands. Tumor cells are further classified by the extent to which they have deviated from the cell of origin: generally, the greater the change, the more unrestrained and dangerous the malignancy.

You may encounter other descriptive labels: classification of cancer is a highly specialized business, undertaken to help physicians provide a more accurate prognosis, or estimate of the likely course of the disease, and to plan their interventions. "Stages" of a malignancy are recognized, depending on the size of the initial tumor, involvement of nearby (local) tissues and lymph glands, and whether metastatic (distant) spread has occurred. Thus Stage I breast cancer means a small, localized breast tumor, and Stage IV means that the breast cancer has spread beyond the local lymph glands to other sites in the body, such as liver, lungs, brain, or bone.

Malignant tumors can have various shapes. They may form a mass, usually with irregular borders, that will protrude if it has developed near the surface of an organ. Or they may appear as a fissure or deep ulcer, or as a cyst-like structure. Sarcomas tend to be larger than carcinomas, to be spindle-shaped, and to merge more with surrounding tissues.

It is estimated that more than one in four North Americans will get cancer, and that about half of those contracting the disease will die of it. Only heart disease is a bigger killer. The combined incidence in the United States and Canada is more than a million new cases a year (excluding non-melanoma skin cancer, which is common but almost always curable). The commonest, and one of the most lethal kinds, is lung cancer, whose incidence in women has increased rapidly because of smoking, overtaking breast cancer as the major malignancy causing death. Cancer of the breast, affecting about one in ten women, is the next most common, followed by cancer of the colon and rectum, the prostate (in men), the uterus (in women), the urinary system, and the blood and lymphoid organs. Cancer is slightly more common in men than in women, and considerably more likely to develop in older people, although many people are affected in their thirties, forties, and fifties, and it is the major cause of death by disease in children aged three to fourteen.

These kinds of statistics can be frightening. However, we are not experiencing an "epidemic" of cancer, as some popular accounts suggest; the overall incidence has not changed much in the last fifty years. Perhaps the main thing to remember is that we are all at risk, but that the risk can be greatly diminished by healthy behaviors.

### How does the body oppose the growth of cancer?

In spite of the efforts of a great many dedicated scientists over many years, we still know very little for certain about the ways in which our bodies normally prevent or retard the development of cancer. The "immune system" is usually cited as our main protection; this term has a particular, rather restricted meaning to the specialist, as I describe below, but is often used more loosely by laypersons to indicate any cancer-opposing mechanisms. It is becoming apparent that, although the immune system does react against some cancers, it is by no means a universal or reliable anti-cancer defense. Other mechanisms in the body work against the disease: for example, circulating hormones influence the growth of some cancers, the growth factors of the specific host tissue probably have an effect, and certain other cells and molecules may play some role. This lack of certainty is undoubtedly very frustrating for the person with cancer who just wants simple answers, but the process of cancer growth and control is, unfortunately, extremely complex.

Let us back up a little and ask a more basic question: Is there evidence that *something* in the body opposes cancer growth, or do these abnormal cells, once formed, simply multiply without restraint? This question is important to us here: if controlling mechanisms do exist, then the disease is likely to be caused, at least in part, by a failure of this control. It would make sense, then, to use treatments based on methods of strengthening the body's control or regulation.

Evidence does exist that development and growth of cancer are normally restrained by controls in the body. First, small "dormant" or "covert" tumors, which apparently do not develop further, are found in normal tissues, for example in the prostate of many men over age forty. These small tumors also show up in the breasts of many women from whom a primary breast cancer has been removed; biopsies (samples of tissue) from the same or opposite breast, or from local lymph glands, often show further small, incipient tumors. We know that these tumors do not ordinarily progress, since many of the people in whom they are found are completely cured by the original surgery.

Another kind of evidence that the spread of cancer is often the result of a failure of control, rather than of an intrinsic property of cancer cells, is the pattern of metastatic growth observed in some cancers. After the removal of a primary breast cancer, there may be no further sign of disease for as long as twenty or thirty years; in a few instances, there can then be a sudden "shower" of metastases, causing death within months. This indicates that cancer cells were present all along but were prevented from further growth by the body, until some unknown set of circumstances occurred that allowed them to escape control.

Indeed, we can be fairly sure that some potential cancer cells exist in all healthy people, since whenever normal cells divide there is a chance of mutation in the DNA; the risk is small in any one cell, but there are so many billions of cells dividing every minute that potentially cancerous ones are constantly being produced. Most cell biologists would agree with this observation, but whereas some would accept that regulatory mechanisms prevent these cells from becoming cancers, others would maintain that we don't all get the disease because each precancerous cell has a very low chance of producing a malignant offspring.

The most dramatic evidence for the view that the body has extensive powers to control at least some cancers comes from the phenomenon of "spontaneous remission," the regression or disappearance of established cancers in the absence of any medical treatment that could possibly account for it. This event is certainly rare, but it now seems that it may be less so than was once thought: a group in the United States has collected accounts of several thousand well-documented cases. We have very little idea what may cause such remissions, and conservative physicians still argue that they are artifacts—the result of faulty initial diagnosis, for example—but many of the cases described have been scrutinized, and their validity has been attested to by experts. This evidence, together with the other observations outlined above, suggests beyond reasonable doubt that the body has considerable cancer-regulating abilities.

What, then, are the mechanisms by which our bodies might prevent cancer or hold it in check once it has developed? I have already mentioned the immune system. The main component of this complex system is a vast army (about a million million) of small, round cells called lymphocytes, which circulate in blood and lymphatic fluid, passing through the tissues and directly attacking or making antibodies against foreign bacteria and viruses that invade us. Our lymph nodes or glands are a part of this system, acting as way-stations in which the lymphocytes can divide; other organs, such as the spleen, bone marrow, and thymus, also contribute to the production and circulation of lymphocytes. There are several kinds of lymphocytes, and you may encounter references to "T cells," some of which directly attack virus-infected cells or tumor cells, and "B cells," which make antibodies, the protective proteins that neutralize antigens, or foreign substances.

This system of defensive cells is the means by which we protect ourselves against infectious organisms, and for many years it has been thought that it is also responsible for destroying cancer cells. Anti-tumor immunity seemed like a natural extension of fighting micro-organisms, since cells from experimental cancers in animals often have on their surfaces novel antigens or substances not found on normal cells; these, we would anticipate, should be treated in the same way as foreign invaders. However, we now know that such tumor antigens are absent in many human cancers. Further, it has been determined that people or animals lacking an effective immune system are not unusually susceptible to the common types of cancers. These facts, plus a number of other observations, make it unlikely that the immune system is our major defense mechanism against malignant disease.

Attention has therefore shifted in many laboratories to the so-called nonspecific immunity mediated by "natural killer" or NK cells and their relatives, which circulate around the body and are capable of killing certain kinds of tumor cells. However, no one yet knows how these NK cells distinguish tumor from normal body cells, and they appear to be ineffective against many types of solid human tumors.

What other defense candidates are there? Hormones, secreted molecules that act as intercellular messengers, are known to affect some tumors. For example, prostatic cancers are often dependent for their growth on male androgens (sex hormones) in the blood, and some breast cancers are stimulated to grow by estrogen or progesterone, the female sex hormones. Therapies based on removing or blocking these hormones frequently shrink or control the growth of corresponding hormone-dependent cancers, but unfortunately such procedures are not effective enough to be curative. Then there is a class of molecules that act locally to control tissue growth, called "growth factors," or locally acting hormones. When normal tissues are developing or spreading, for example to heal a wound, they need ways of signaling to their constituent cells when it is time to stop multiplying. Sensitivity to such signals may, however, be lost as cells progress toward a cancerous state. In addition to these circulating and local hormones, other kinds of molecules are cited from time to time as possible cancer controllers.

You will see that, unfortunately, we are simply not sure yet what regulates cancer cells. A reasonable position, given present knowledge, would be that there are indeed normal body defenses against cancer; early cancerous changes in cells can often be repaired by intracellular enzymes, and aberrant cells restrained by local hormones; then, at later stages along the path toward cancer, the dangerous cells may be recognized and killed by both classical and "natural" immune mechanisms.

Now we have the background to see why it has been necessary to belabor this rather technical issue. There are two very different points of view about the conditions that allow cancer to grow in the body. The first places all the blame on the cancer cells themselves and downplays or denies any significant role for the defenses of the "host." This is still the prevailing idea behind most current medical treatment of cancer: it leads to the concept that we need to "get it all" or remove absolutely all abnormal cells when performing surgery, irradiation, or chemotherapy, even though this is probably impossible, since cells inevitably spread through the body in the circulation. This philosophy also denies a role to adjunctive or supplementary techniques that attempt to strengthen the innate capacity of body and mind to resist the disease.

The second, newer, point of view is that cancer is caused as much by a failure of these normal regulatory mechanisms that we have discussed above as by changes intrinsic to the malignant cells. How does this help us? It helps because it provides a second avenue for treatment. If inadequate regulation is a promoting factor, then we can *strengthen* that regulation. How? Eventually we may know enough to do it by injection of chemical agents that make the normal controls in the body work more efficiently. For the present we don't know how to do this, but we do know something that will help us, which is the central idea in this book: we know that the *mind,* or the brain, is the master regulator of the body (more about this in Chapter 5). We can work with our minds to improve conditions in the body so that the cancer will find it very difficult or impossible to grow. You might think of it like this: the cancer has learned to grow in the "soup" that the body provides. If you want to help your body resist the growth of cancer, then there need to be changes in this soup. The direction of these changes is towards harmony, peace, relaxation, absence of undue stress and conflict. Spiritual growth is important also as we will discuss later. As the mind changes in this way, so it will signal the body that all is well, and the soup will return to a composition that is the best possible for restraining cancer growth, or any other disease for that matter.

## What eventually happens to people with cancer?

The first thing to be reiterated here is that a diagnosis of cancer does not necessarily mean death; about half of us survive! Outcome depends on a number of factors: the stage of the disease when it is diagnosed, its site in the body, the kinds of mutations that have taken place in the cancer cells, and the general health and resistance of the patient. Advanced metastatic cancer is, of course, very serious and almost always fatal. Death may come from damage to the vital organs, from complications caused by treatments, or from "cancer cachexia," a gradual starving of the normal tissues as the more rapidly dividing cancer cells consume available nutrients.

The physician faces an unenviable task when communicating with patients whose disease has reached the terminal stages. Some patients ask: "How long do I have?" Others deeply resent or are depressed by being given a time. In any case, it is often extremely difficult to estimate how long someone will live; the course of cancer can vary greatly. Survival statistics are averages and may not reflect the prospects of a patient determined to fight and to do everything possible to help himself or herself. In accordance with the prevailing biomedical view that cancer is governed purely by biological factors, such characteristics of the patient tend to be ignored when predictions about outcome are made.

There is often an understandable fear among patients that death from cancer will be accompanied by unbearable pain, so it is comforting to know that, in the majority of cases, physical pain can be adequately controlled by modern drugs. Emotional pain is another matter; in our society, we generally leave patient and family to deal with it by themselves, and it has been my observation that, at most stages of the disease, many people suffer more from having to face the implications of their mortality than they do from physical changes in the body. Much of what I discuss in the later chapters of this book has a bearing on the relief of emotional pain. Remarkably, quality of life can remain high up to the time of death.

## Summary

In this chapter, I briefly described the cellular events underlying cancer, then reviewed some of the lifestyle and environmental factors that are known to promote the disease, and discussed the various clinical types of cancer and their frequency of occurrence. In response to the question of how the body protects itself, we discovered that views are changing as a result of modern research in cell biology. Cancer was formerly thought to be a completely self-contained invader, resulting from a rare genetic accident and growing independently of its host; now we know it is more accurately seen as an aberration of cell growth that is usually held in check by a variety of normal defense mechanisms. The importance of this shift in ideas is that, as well as trying to kill the cancer cells, it now appears rational to use therapies designed to strengthen our own defenses.

## Part Two

# Help From
# Outside

# 3 The Benefits and Limitations of Medical Treatment

There are many ways to assist healing. We are most familiar with one approach: the administration of certain kinds of medication and the performance of certain procedures that we lump together under the term "Western medicine." Different approaches have been used in other cultures and at other times. In attempting to survey the whole field of assisted healing, we may subdivide its philosophies in various ways: in this book, I have drawn a distinction between external and internal routes to healing, that is, between attempts to reverse disease by applying agents and procedures from outside, and efforts made by the patient to mobilize his or her internal resources to heal from within. Our aim is to explain and justify adding the latter to our treatment of cancer. In the process, we need an overview of what can be done for cancer patients from the outside, some appraisal of the strengths and weaknesses of the external route to healing for cancer patients—since it is assumed by many to be the only valid approach.

Treatment from outside may be further divided into two categories: conventional Western biomedicine (the subject of this chapter) and procedures and agents that are "unconventional," that is, used primarily in cultures other than ours, or used in the West but without any evidence of their efficacy (discussed in the next chapter). It may seem sacrilegious to link modern Western medicine and unorthodox or unproven remedies, but they have some properties in common. They both encourage us to place our fate in the hands of someone else, a designated "healer," or to rely on his or her remedies. They draw much of their appeal from our tendency to regress under the extreme threat of serious illness, to want somebody or something, a substitute parent perhaps, to "make it better" or take the problem away. I am not making a case for the use of unproven remedies, as will become obvious in the next chapter, nor denying that conventional medicine has an important, indeed predominant, role in cancer treatment. However, it is appropriate here, before we move to a consideration of healing from within, to review briefly the main facts about our current major conventional forms of treatment, and the implications of relying exclusively on them.

## Diagnostic methods

There is no single, general test for the presence of cancer. Nevertheless, an array of powerful procedures can be used to confirm what is suspected after a clinical examination. These procedures include radiological techniques (both the familiar X-rays and more sophisticated techniques such as CAT-scanning, which can provide cross-sectional images of the body); imaging with ultrasound (sound waves); endoscopy (flexible tubes inserted into orifices, for viewing or biopsy); tracking the distribution of injected radioactive isotopes; and blood tests to detect abnormal circulating molecules. Final confirmation of the diagnosis often comes from histological (microscopic) examination of cells taken from the suspected cancer itself (biopsy), although this, like all diagnostic procedures, is not by any means infallible. As is the case in many areas of medicine, however, the diagnostic arm of oncology, the specialty dealing with cancer, is basically superb, sensitive, and reliable; it would be irrational and often harmful not to take advantage of it.

When cancer has been diagnosed, should the patient be told? There has been a dramatic shift in this practice in North America. Until about twenty years ago, few physicians explicitly told their patients about the diagnosis; now the great majority do so, although this is still uncommon in many other countries. This change in community attitude has profound implications for the way we cope with the disease; it allows individuals to confront their situation realistically, to cooperate in planning their own treatment, and if life is likely to be short, to plan to use the remaining time as productively as possible.

## Types of treatment

In contrast to achievements in diagnosis, Western medical treatments for cancer, particularly for advanced cancer, are very far from ideal, and in many instances are ineffective and harmful to the patient. It is customary to emphasize the successes of medical treatment for cancer, and I do not want to belittle these, especially since my own life was saved by surgery. However, when we look at the field as a whole it becomes obvious that cancer medicine is still in a rather primitive state compared with treatments for many other disease conditions. The three major types of treatments are surgery, radiation therapy, and chemotherapy, all rather crude techniques that damage normal tissues as well as the cancer. In time we will probably develop much more subtle and effective external methods, based on manipulation of the way the body naturally regulates and prevents abnormal growth.

When cancer is in the early stages and is localized, there is, of course, the best chance of cure, surgery being the usual method employed. The hope is to remove all of the primary tumor and adjacent normal tissue into which cancerous cells may have spread. The local lymph nodes are often excised as well, since in many cancers, cells that detach from the tumor accumulate there and would subsequently multiply and circulate throughout the body. However, as noted earlier, it is probably impossible to remove from the body *all* the cancerous cells that originated in a particular tumor; nonetheless, it makes sense to get rid of as many as possible, so that the body's own regulatory mechanisms may more easily control or remove the remainder.

Ionizing radiation (gamma rays and high-energy photons) is the preferred treatment when cancers cannot be conveniently or safely removed with surgical procedures; for example, tumors of the larynx are irradiated to avoid damage to the vocal chords. Irradiation may also be used as an adjunct to surgery; in cases of breast cancer, the surgical site is irradiated to kill locally surviving cancer cells. Radiation is also extremely useful for palliative treatment of metastatic cancer in structures like bone (palliative treatment or care is designed to ease distress without any expectation of cure). Modern developments allow relatively accurate focusing of the radiation beam, but, inevitably, some normal cells in the vicinity are destroyed as well.

The third main cancer treatment mode is chemotherapy, a term covering a wide variety of injected or ingested drugs that kill dividing cells. Since cancer cells are dividing constantly, being dangerous for that reason, they are more susceptible than most normal tissues to these agents. Chemotherapeutic drugs, unlike surgery or radiation, can seek out cancer cells throughout the body. This ability might seem to make them the ideal treatment for disseminated cancer, but unfortunately they seldom, if ever, can be used at high enough doses to remove all the abnormal cells because such high doses have a lethal effect on normal cells that are also dividing—on the cells lining the intestines, for example. Chemotherapeutic drugs, singly or in combinations, have proven very effective against certain cancers—for example, testicular cancer, Hodgkin's lymphoma, and leukemias in children, in all of which they often bring about complete cures. Unfortunately, the available drugs do not cure advanced stages of the common cancers of lung, breast, and digestive tract. Chemotherapy was first used as a mode of treatment in the 1940s, and intensive research is being done on developing new drugs and combinations of them. Thus, we can hope for further advances.

This brief account of the major current medical treatments for cancer may be supplemented, for those wanting more detail, by reading some of the references in "Further Reading." We have enough background now to make an evaluation of the benefits and limitations of medical treatment.

## Making treatment decisions

Early-stage cancer can often be cured, particularly by surgery; for example, the success rate is high with cancer of the breast or bowel. It is therefore foolish not to seek medical advice and treatment as early as possible when cancer is suspected. People often delay going to their doctors when they find a lump or unexplained bleeding; their subconscious fear is so great that a kind of magical thinking takes over: "If I ignore this, it will just go away." As a result of such wishful thinking, many lives are lost unnecessarily. (I want to emphasize again here that even when a localized cancer is "completely" removed by surgery, there is usually considerable risk of recurrence, from cells that escaped before or during the surgical procedure. Therefore the self-help approaches that we will describe later are not at all irrelevant in such situations, but should be used to diminish the likelihood of such a recurrence.)

Advanced cancer is a different matter. We need, first, to get a clear picture of what we are up against, which means availing ourselves of the great diagnostic power of modern medicine. When it comes to treatment planning, however, patients who wish to help themselves have to do more than passively accept their physician's recommendations. We can list the steps one might take:

(a) Clarify what you want and expect. Most of us would unhesitatingly say we want to be "cured," which seems to mean that the disease should be eliminated and the status quo restored. While it is natural to hope for this, it is important to realize that "cure" is usually not achievable if cancer has become widespread. A more realistic goal is to live as long as possible in good health. In some cases, if a person is free of disease for several years after treatment, his or her risk of further disease falls to a level no greater than that of others in the population, which we could reasonably term a "cure."

(b) Find out what the treatment options are. We need to know how effective various types of treatments are, and what the most advanced medical thinking is on the subject. Sometimes, the benefits of treatment are clear-cut; often they are not. A second opinion may be sought, and physicians sometimes disagree about the best course of action. When this happens, it is usually because it is difficult, even for an expert, to predict with confidence the course of the disease and the effects of treatment.

(c) Determine what the likely side-effects of treatment may be. Sometimes these are severe. For chemotherapy, they may include nausea, vomiting, increased susceptibility to infections, hair loss, mouth sores, diarrhea, and injuries to internal organs.

(d) Acknowledge that everyone—you, your doctor, and your family—wants to do *something*. That is, we may feel reassured if some treatment is being administered, whether or not it helps. The agonizing task of the actively involved patient is to balance possible benefits against the probable loss of some quality of life if treatment is taken.

(e) Accept that medicine cannot yet cure most advanced cancers; the best that it can offer in most cases is palliation. This is important because it is tempting to pin all our hopes on external intervention, even when we are told that the chances of benefit are small. This seemingly harmless and comforting strategy is employed by many, perhaps most, patients. Its great drawback, as I have observed in hundreds of cases, is that total reliance on external help may prevent us from coming to grips with what is really happening, from facing squarely the threat of death, recognizing that our time may be short, and doing whatever we feel is most important in our lives while we are able to, including repairing

relationships and trying to help ourselves with the kinds of techniques I describe later.
(f) Work out a strategy of self-help to complement your medical treatment.

These last two points may seem to be asking a lot of people with a life-threatening disease; we all want something to cling to when our lives are in danger. Yet Western medical practice—or, more fairly, Western society, which demands that diseases be cured by external interventions—keeps patients passive and prevents us from learning what we can from illness. This idea, that illness has something to teach us, and a related one, that we can often, by our own efforts, make a difference, represents a point of view that has been adopted by some in our culture, but not yet by the majority. It is also a philosophy that is susceptible to abuse, as is made clear in later chapters. Here I want simply to emphasize the fact that we cannot rely on medicine at its current stage of evolution as the exclusive treatment for cancer. It makes sense to use it as the first line of defense, but we must actively participate in the struggle.

## The search for new treatments

Establishing the effectiveness of a new drug or procedure is a long and costly process; it is frustrating and often incomprehensible to the patient, who wants to know why he or she can't be treated, right now, with something that seems promising. Understanding some basic facts about testing procedures may help us understand why it takes so long, and will also provide useful background to the discussion, in the next chapter, on how to evaluate "unproven" remedies.

The first task with a new drug or other treatment is to establish how toxic it is, how much of it can be administered without doing undue harm. Toxicity is usually tested first with animals, then later with informed human volunteers. The next step is to determine whether the tumor is affected when the drug is administered at a

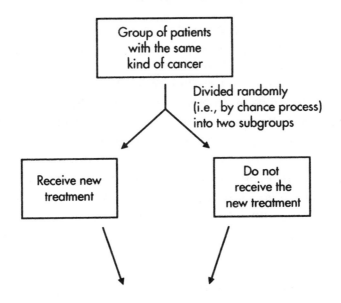

Figure 3
*The procedure followed in a randomized controlled trial for testing the effects of a new treatment.*

dose level that is not seriously toxic. Finally, if possible, a "randomized controlled study" is done, comparing the anti-tumor effect of the new drug with that of the best extant treatment, to see if the new one is better.

The rationale of a randomized controlled trial is simple (see Figure 3). Ideally, one would like to compare how the patient would respond to the new drug and to the old (current, standard) treatment. Obviously, administering both to the same person would not be instructive: it would be impossible to tell which drug was responsible for any effects. As an alternative, a group of, say, two hundred similar patients is divided *randomly*—that is, by a chance process like a coin toss—into two equal groups of a hundred. One group gets the new drug or treatment; the other receives the standard treatment. Because the groups are formed by random selection, we can assume that they are the same, that is, that the average response of each group to either treatment would be closely similar. Thus, the effects of the two treatments, the new and the old, can be compared by seeing whether the tumor grows more slowly in the patients getting the new treatment, or whether, on average, they live longer.

This rather involved procedure would not be necessary if new drugs or agents were overwhelmingly better than what is currently considered to be best; such an advantage would be quickly obvious to physicians. However, this virtually never happens, and even when a new agent seems to have miraculous healing powers, a properly controlled trial almost always shows that its advantages are either modest or nonexistent. This is why it is difficult to draw reliable conclusions from simply observing the effects of a new treatment on a small number of patients, and why most physicians are reluctant to recommend unproven therapies to patients. It also explains, to anticipate the next chapter, why controlled studies of popularly touted "remedies" are essential before these are presented to the public.

New drugs and combinations of them are constantly being made and tested in these ways. What is perhaps more exciting is that extensive testing is being undertaken of a range of new nondrug agents and procedures, often lumped together in the category of "biological response modifiers." Such treatments, which attempt to enhance the body's own tumor-regulating powers, include:

• *Interferon*: The interferons are a family of proteins, discovered in 1957, that have anti-viral properties and also regulate cell division. Premature claims through the media raised expectations unduly when they were first used to treat cancer a few years ago. After intensive testing it has been found that interferon causes temporary dramatic remissions in some (rare) malignancies of blood-forming cells, and has smaller effects on certain other cancers and limited or no effects on the common ones.

• *Monoclonal antibodies*: A dream of cancer therapists since the turn of the century has been to find a "magic bullet" that would home in on tumor cells, killing them and leaving normal cells unscathed. The dream has been revived because of the development of ways to make purified (monoclonal) antibodies at very high concentration, which can, at times, seek out and combine specifically with tumor cells, although without killing them in most cases. There have been attempts to exploit the homing properties of these antibodies by first attaching to them toxic agents—drugs or radioactive isotopes—and allowing the monoclonal antibodies to carry their cell-killing passenger molecules directly to the tumor cells. With a few rare exceptions, this procedure has not yet led to effective anticancer therapy.

• *Tumor vaccines*: The concept of immunizing people against their own tumors has long been attractive to immunologists. This was attempted by removing tumors from a patient, grinding them up, adding certain bacterial products, and administering the mixture to the same patient. The procedure showed some early promise, but long-term results have been disappointing.

• *Growth factors*: I have previously mentioned these locally acting hormones, which are known to be important regulators of the growth and differentiation of many kinds of cells. The hope is that we may learn how to administer them so as to persuade tumor cells to change from their usual primitive, proliferating, and therefore dangerous form into more differentiated "end cells"; a transition from uncontrollable adolescence to stable adulthood. Trials of this idea are still at an early stage.

• *Interleukin-2 and adoptive cellular therapy*: Interleukin-2 is a molecule that makes some kinds of immune cells divide; when white cells (lymphocytes) are drawn from the blood and incubated with interleukin in a test tube, they become "activated" and will more vigorously attack a tumor when returned to the body, especially if more interleukin is injected with them. Some promising responses have been obtained against melanoma (malignant skin cancer), colorectal carcinoma, and Hodgkin's lymphoma. A recent advance has been to use lymphocytes that have infiltrated the patient's own tumor in place of blood cells; the idea is that these cells have a particular affinity for the tumor, but need activation by the interleukin before they will effectively attack the tumor cells. This work is very new, and it will take some years to test the methods for therapeutic value.

• *Genetic engineering:* In the last chapter, I mentioned the changes in the genes (DNA) that render cells cancerous. This is a multi-stage process: some genes (proto-oncogenes) must be activated, others (tumor-suppressor genes) "turned off." In the long term, we may learn to manipulate these genetic events so as to prevent harmful changes and encourage those genes that protect cells against malignant transformation.

Will any of these new kinds of therapies lead to a "cure" for cancer? The experts in cellular and molecular biology of cancer are not claiming that any such cure is imminent, but more effective drugs will no doubt gradually be discovered, and ways of strengthening the body's own defenses will become more sophisticated. This last approach, sometimes called "the fourth modality of cancer treatment" (surgery, radiation, and chemotherapy being the first three), is the most appealing because it aims at control of cancer cells without killing normal cells. It is also of interest to us here because any effect the mind may have on cancer will presumably act through these internal defense mechanisms, as I discuss in Chapter 5. However, notwithstanding such upbeat slogans as "Cancer can be beaten," used by fundraising agencies, we must recognize that cancer is not comparable to infections, which can be reversed simply by administering the right antibiotic. Cancer represents a failure of the body's own regulation, an internal breakdown rather than an assault from without. In my opinion, it is likely that as long as there are bodies they will get cancer, and that in many cases, the disease will remain difficult to cure.

## Summary

We have briefly surveyed what modern Western biomedicine can do to treat cancer. While increasingly sophisticated diagnostic techniques have come into use, and surgical or other interventions for early-stage cancers are often curative, it has to be admitted that currently available methods for treating advanced cancer are still largely ineffective and often harmful to the patient. A diagnosis of metastatic cancer demands a number of very difficult decisions from the patient; treatment options must be explored, the possible side-effects clarified, and the likelihood of premature death accepted.

The procedures used to test new drugs were briefly described. Some areas of current research into biological methods of augmenting the body's own defenses hold promise, but it does not seem likely that any of these will yield a general "cure" for all cancers in the near future.

# 4 Evaluating Unorthodox Therapies

Because cancer poses such a threat to life, and because medicine cannot guarantee a cure, many of us who have been diagnosed as having cancer look around for additional, nonmedical remedies, in the hope of improving our chances of survival. When we do this we encounter numerous confusing and often conflicting claims for the curative effects of a great variety of external agents and procedures. These may be described as "alternatives," implying that they can take the place of traditional medical treatments or procedures, or as "complementary" or "adjunctive" treatments, to be added to medical treatments and procedures. How can we know whether any of them have value?

In this Chapter I will offer some general guidelines on the evaluation of such unconventional remedies, directing my remarks again at agents and procedures applied from outside. (The mobilizing of internal resources, "healing from within," which is also unconventional to most people, will be dealt with in subsequent chapters.) Before proceeding, however, I should acknowledge some limitations in my own experience. My original training and research were in Western biomedical science, with additional training and experience in psychology and introspective techniques; I have no significant professional or personal experience with the medicines of other cultures or with most of the unproven external remedies I will discuss, although I have known many people who have tried some of them. Thus I will be able to look at these treatments only from the external viewpoint of a Western scientist.

## Examples of unconventional treatments

Particular unorthodox treatments tend to be popular for a number of years and then to be displaced by different ones (a phenomenon also seen in regular medicine). Dr. Barrie Cassileth, a leading researcher in this area, has published a useful list and critique of the "alternatives" most popular in the United States since 1800.[1] Early in the last century, emetics and hot baths were favored. Later in the century, homeopathy was a predominant medical philosophy and was applied to cancer; it was not "unorthodox" at that time, although it certainly is seen to be so now. Homeopathic physicians administer minute amounts of a wide variety of substances to patients, the specific drug used depending on an elaborate written compilation of remedies for various symptoms of bodily disharmony. Naturopathy, osteopathy, and chiropractic were in vogue at the turn of the century as cancer treatments, and all are still used, at least as adjuncts, for cancer patients and for those with many other diseases. Naturopathy, which avoids the use of drugs, emphasizes the fact that health is dependent on being in balance with natural laws; osteopathy and chiropractic use manipulation of the spine to cure imbalances in the body.

In the early twentieth century, a number of tablet and ointment cancer cures were popular. In the 1920s, there were treatments based on "energy," such as radio waves and light. In the 1940s, Koch's glyoxylide (distilled water) was used; it was displaced in the 1950s by Hoxsey's remedy, a mixture of herbal products; in the 1960s, by krebiozen (mineral oil); and in the 1970s by Laetrile, an extract of apricot pits.

In another study,[2] Dr. Cassileth found the current most popular unorthodox remedies in the United States to be (in order of popularity):

1. "Metabolic" therapy, a group of treatments, each of which includes several elements: "detoxification" (often through colonic irrigation), special diets, and intake of vitamins and minerals. A well-known example is the Gerson regimen.
2. Diet therapy, involving diet alone. The macrobiotic diet is a predominant example.
3. Megavitamin therapy, in which very high doses of one or several vitamins are administered.
4. Mental imaging for anti-tumor effects.
5. Spiritual or faith healing, often involving prayer and laying-on of hands, with the aim of obtaining divine intervention.
6. "Immune" therapy, the injection of serum fractions, vaccines from the patients' own tumors, fetal tissues, and other materials aimed at stimulating the immune system.

There are dozens more, including Essiac, wheat-grass therapy, the Kelley nutritional program, Iscador, Antineoplastons, the Livingstone-Wheeler vaccine, eumetabolic treatment, dimethyl-sulphoxide, hydrazine sulphate, and many others. Different countries have their own: for example, pau d'Arco, from the bark of trees, is offered in Argentina, and extract of birch ash is the most common unproven remedy in Finland.

The agents listed above are not part of any coherent medical philosophy. However, there are many therapeutic systems that have been in existence for hundreds or even thousands of years, which we in the West would also classify as unorthodox, for example, Ayurvedic (Asian Indian) and traditional Chinese medicines. These systems are based on world views and methods of establishing validity that differ from our own. Presumably many, and probably the great majority, of the world's cancer patients have been treated by such "alternative" practices. I believe that these long-standing bodies of knowledge must not be dismissed, but I cannot comment on their efficacy, and must refer the interested reader to accounts such as those by Kaptchuk and Croucher.[3] As far as I know, there are no published Western studies of the impact on cancer patients of established traditional treatment methods from other cultures, although Chinese herbal medicines are currently being evaluated. My comments in this chapter are directed mainly at the more transient alternative remedies that have been used in our own society.

What are we to make of the great variety of treatments that have been proposed? I will discuss methods of evaluating purported cures in a moment, but some common-sense observations may be offered here on the phenomenon of alternative remedies in general. First, since many of the claims are contradictory, they can't all be valid; for example, diets based on cooked grains, and others insisting that all food must be consumed raw, are at loggerheads. Second, the incredible variety and diversity of these "alternatives" might reasonably cause us to wonder if any of them is useful, since if any one had proved its efficacy, the rest would very likely have faded from popularity. Third, there is usually a great deal of emotion surrounding the promotion of a popular alternative remedy, and we have to wonder why this is necessary—why the product's effects can't speak for themselves. And, finally, an attack on organized medicine, with charges of a "conspiracy" to suppress alternatives, is often associated with the promotion of specific unconventional agents. This seems absurd: all of us are liable to cancer and would be only too pleased if a simple remedy could be found. One has to suspect that such charges, and the excessive emotionalism, conceal a basic insecurity in the advocates' positions.

## Who uses unorthodox remedies, and why?

Roughly a third of cancer patients use complementary or alternative medicines[4]. The numbers seem to have increased in the last 10 years, and the climate of medical opinion about them is gradually changing—towards the view that at least some of these agents and procedures deserve investigation. Earlier there was concern that individuals taking alternative treatments were ignorant, desperate people, who abandoned medical treatment for unproven remedies. Now, thanks to a spate of recent research, it is clear that those seeking such help are relatively resourceful and well educated, and that the unorthodox help is added to, not substituted for, medical treatment. In fact, though it is a simple matter to present oneself regularly at a medical clinic for treatment, it takes a degree of self-assertion and initiative to seek out additional help, a willingness to be involved in one's recovery, and a belief that one's own actions can make a difference. Alternative treatments are sometimes expensive, and are not usually covered by health insurance; travel may be necessary to seek out a particular treatment regimen. Thus, people need to be flexible, active, and determined to go beyond the culturally sanctioned treatment modes.

Why would capable individuals pin their hopes on apparently illogical and unproven remedies? The most potent motivation is probably fear of death; rational thinking tends to be suspended when one's life is threatened. Then there is often a need to find someone who will pay attention to all aspects of our experience of having cancer; busy medical clinics are usually interested only in physical symptoms, while proponents of alternatives may be concerned with many aspects of our lifestyle, including the psychological, social, and spiritual. Related to this is the intense anger many patients feel at the threat to life and plans. This anger is often channeled toward physicians, and seeking out alternative practitioners can be an expression of protest. The remedies offered by unorthodox therapists are frequently, although not always, more appealing because they are often less toxic and painful than conventional anti-cancer agents and procedures. Anything involving food tends to invoke the connections we made in early childhood between eating and comfort. Beyond that, we all have a tendency to believe what we want to believe, a tendency especially pronounced in times of crisis, and the confident pronouncements of alternative therapists may be more comforting in the short run, for people with serious disease, than the responsible though dispiriting pessimism of the medical profession. Finally, much of the current counterculture wisdom about cancer treatment is, at least superficially, rooted in a philosophy of getting back to nature, attending to the whole person, seeking balance and harmony in life, and rejecting what is seen as a bloodless, big-business, high-tech, and dehumanized approach to medical care. There is, I believe, some justification for this stance, although it is often adopted in an irrational and highly emotional way.

## How can we evaluate remedies?

There are three main things to look for in forming an opinion on the effectiveness of any treatment, whether conventional or unorthodox: evidence, rationale, and consensus. Let us examine these one by one.

The strongest *evidence* we can have for the effectiveness of an agent comes from a randomized controlled trial, as explained in the last chapter. Other less rigorous kinds of experiments exist, but the best depend on some comparison between matched groups of patients, only one of which receives the treatment. The next-best type of evidence is "correlative"; that is, there is a consistent association between giving the treatment and a beneficial effect, as observed by qualified practitioners. It is vital, of course, that people assessing a new procedure be appropriately trained to do so, and at least reasonably impartial. Anecdotal evidence alone—relating stories about selected patients—cannot be conclusive; if one hundred dying patients take a new treatment and one of them survives, an anecdote about that person alone may sound impressive. However, if we learn that the other ninety-nine died, it is much less impressive. In "popular" reports we usually do not hear about these others. When survival is a rare event, we need to rule out other possible causes, such as misdiagnosis. Unfortunately, most of the "alternative" health community, and many journalists, rely mainly on anecdotal reports.

The data on tests of a new procedure must also be made publicly available. Generally, test data and a complete description of the experimental procedures are published as a journal article, which allows others to assess the validity of the test and to attempt to replicate it. Vague assertions and personal testimonials that appear in popular magazines simply have no validity. Objective tests must be done to eliminate human bias and wishful thinking. The history of alternative cancer therapy, and of medicine in general, is full of examples of individuals strongly advocating a "new therapy," often refusing to let others test it or to divulge its contents, and then finally being exposed as dishonest or mistaken when an examination by dispassionate observers was completed.

The second thing to look for is *rationale*; that is, does the reputed effect of the treatment make sense according to some organized scheme of knowledge? Many Western scientists require that this organized scheme be current biomedical theory; I would be less demanding, since I believe that we have not yet reached any kind of final understanding of biology, and that novel effects are possible. Nevertheless, it helps greatly to know how an agent might plausibly work; if we don't, the evidence needs to be strong. If both evidence and rationale are lacking, as is often the case, there is little reason to take a claim seriously.

The third criterion by which to judge whether a treatment works is to see if there is a *consensus* among informed people. This can only be an indication: experts can be wrong. When a patient asks for a second opinion, he or she is, in effect, testing the consensus of medical opinion, and it sometimes happens that conflicting advice is given, indicating that there is no certainty about the patient's specific situation. If there is no consensus about a new treatment, but, instead, a plethora of conflicting claims, as is the case with dietary cures for cancer, we can fairly be skeptical of individual advocates.

There are other criteria you can apply in your evaluation of therapies: is there secrecy, a highly emotional atmosphere surrounding the procedure, or is a lot of money at stake? Is a gratuitous attack on the medical establishment associated with the treatment? But I think you will find that if you enquire about the three major criteria—evidence, rationale, and consensus—you will quickly see whether an unfamiliar treatment should be taken seriously.

## How do psychological techniques compare with unorthodox external remedies?

In much of the literature analyzing "alternatives," psychological techniques such as mental imaging are lumped together with unproven external remedies, like megavitamins and immune-enhancement or dietary cures. This may be justified when mental imaging or positive thinking is used in an isolated, rote-learning kind of way, which is very different from integrating such techniques into a comprehensive self-help plan. However, a clear distinction should be made between responsible psychological self-help and the irrational remedies that we have been discussing here. We will discuss, in later chapters, evidence for effects of psychological therapy on lifespan. A rationale for such effects can also be perceived, at least in outline. I would therefore wish to distance this approach from the use of external remedies that lack evidence or rationale.

Systematic psychological help for cancer patients is by now considered orthodox if its aim is to alleviate distress, but still unorthodox if used to prolong life. You should be aware that many mental health professionals still do not take seriously the claim that psychological interventions can prolong life in some cancer patients.

## What effects do unorthodox treatments have?

The majority of unorthodox remedies are agents that do not belong to any coherent philosophy of treatment or have any credible mechanism of action; each of these remedies is being advocated, not universally, but by a special-interest group. Examples include Laetrile, Krebiozen, the Hoxsey remedy, megavitamins, and many of the more exotic dietary regimens—for example, eating only grapes for a time—and food additives. When we apply the three major evaluation criteria to these procedures, we find no reason to believe that any of them is effective: there is no scientific evidence, no rationale, and no consensus. Laetrile and vitamin C, for example, have been tested in controlled trials (most of the others have not) and found to have no life-prolonging effect. There is also no rationale that makes sense; for example, to explain the action of Laetrile, it is claimed, without evidence, that cancer cells, but not normal cells, contain a special enzyme that releases cyanide from Laetrile when it enters the cell, killing it. Although this agent was widely touted some years ago, and is still used, it has been largely displaced by other favorites in North America, and one has to wonder why, if it is as effective as has been claimed. For more information about this subject you could consult medical sources[5][6] in the "Notes" at the back of the book, or for a more optimistic account by a social scientist, consult Michael Lerner's excellent book *Choices in Healing*.[7]

A second category of unorthodox procedures consists of the treatment of cancer according to "unconventional" systems of medicine: traditional Chinese medicine, for example, or homeopathy. The usual establishment response is to dismiss such systems out of hand. I prefer to reserve judgment; these approaches, and others like them, often have a well-worked-out theory (rationale) supporting them, even if this is unfamiliar to the Western mind, and they have often been used for a very long time (indicating some consensus). The macrobiotic diet, for example, is advocated as part of an attempt to bring the individual into balance and harmony with nature. It seems fair, however, to ask that, if these systems are advocated as cancer treatments within our culture, they be subject to the same kinds of experimental testing done on conventional agents.

Potentially harmful effects of unproven remedies include the possibility that they may produce toxicity in the patient. For example, some vitamins are toxic in high doses (A, D, and E); frequent colonic irrigation has attendant dangers; unsterilized needles used in unlicensed "immunotherapy clinics" may transmit infections; unorthodox diets may cause nutritional deficiencies, which is especially hazardous for cancer patients, who may need the protein. At the psychological and social levels, patients may be put to unnecessary expense by purchasing remedies or services not covered by health insurance, and their lives may be disrupted by traveling to distant clinics or by having to prepare and eat only special foods. As well, there is disappointment when ineffective remedies fail to work; orthodox critics have much to say about this, decrying the "false hope" generated by alternatives. (See Chapter 7 for discussion of this contentious issue.)

The impact of these complementary therapies, even when they are ineffective, is by no means all bad, however. "False hope" is a curious expression: hope itself is always uplifting; "false" is a qualifier added by an outsider who judges that this hope is unwarranted, but, even if that is true, the immediate benefits of having something to pin one's hopes on may outweigh the eventual pain of disappointment. I have observed that many people are quite capable of being hopeful about a remedy, and thereby alleviating anxiety, while simultaneously not really being surprised that the remedy does little good. Simply having something one can do, some sense of control over events, can be very reassuring. And we can by no means rule out a real physical effect through the influence of belief and positive mood on the body. The placebo effect is well established: many physical changes, including the documented relief of such diseases as arthritis and gastrointestinal ulcers, or of symptoms such as pain and nausea, have come about in patients who were given substances such as sugar pills or injections of distilled water while believing these to be effective medications. Finally, we must have the humility to acknowledge that things happen that we don't yet understand. Acupuncture was derided for years in the West but is now accepted as having real effects on some conditions, although the mechanisms that produce those effects are not clear to us. Research may show that other alternative treatments, too, are effective.

## Who advocates unorthodox remedies, and why?

Many patients these days are subjected to a great deal of advice from well-meaning friends and relatives, who are driven to suggest something in order to alleviate their own anxiety. Their ideas often come from the numerous presentations on unconventional therapies put out by the mass media. The person with cancer may be forced to tell friends that what he or she needs instead is support and caring. Some advocates are simply unscrupulous, exploiting people for profit, although their numbers are dwindling in the face of a better-informed and more sophisticated consumer market. A third, and more prevalent group includes a broad spectrum of advocates, ranging from apparently well-qualified people such as physicians, through "psychotherapists" of various backgrounds, to individuals with irrelevant degrees, and recovered patients and others with strong emotional needs to promote alternatives.

The first thing the patient seeking help must do is ascertain whether the "advocate" has truly relevant qualifications and experience: having recovered from cancer oneself is not sufficient grounds for knowing what might help others, and the title "psychotherapist" can be used by anyone. Second, it is important to find out whether any claims made for a mode of treatment are supported by documented evidence (not simply by assertions or anecdotes), and to determine, perhaps by consulting other professionals, whether there is some rationale for the treatment and some consensus about it. I know this is difficult for the desperate cancer patient, who may want just to leave everything to a charismatic figure. Yet if this procedure is followed, almost all of the advocacy on special diets or remedies, often recommended by apparent experts, will be seen to be without foundation.

Why do some professionals advocate unproven and almost certainly ineffective remedies? Sometimes they do so for profit, but in my experience, and as Dr. Cassileth found, it tends to be done with sincerity. Clinical professionals don't necessarily have training in relevant specialties, and may be genuinely naive. Physicians and psychologists, for example, usually have little training in nutrition, but may feel tempted to make pronouncements in this area because they are accustomed to being looked up to for advice. There are some interesting psychological mechanisms at work here: if we are well paid and perceived as powerful, then we tend to adjust our beliefs to suit our perception of ourselves as knowledgeable and important; thus we may give advice in areas we know little about. And if we find the uncertainty surrounding cancer hard to tolerate, and our impotence to help unbearable, or if our own fear of death is unrecognized within us, then we may find it easiest to take a more dogmatic stance in recommending treatments to people than is warranted by the evidence. These influences are usually subconscious, and can be at work in orthodox and unorthodox therapists alike.

## Summary

We have surveyed the area of unorthodox therapies for cancer, dealing mainly with those remedies that are externally administered and unconnected to any coherent theory of healing. We noted that there has been a great variety of remedies advocated: for example, "metabolic" therapies, dietary cures, "immune" therapies, megavitamins, and specific mixtures or compounds like Laetrile, the Hoxsey herbal mixture, krebiozen, and various vaccines and chemicals. Most have been popular for a limited time only. These procedures and agents are generally used as adjuncts, and not as alternatives, to regular medical treatments. They tend to be employed by people who are resourceful rather than ignorant. These individuals may be driven by fear of dying, by a desire to satisfy psychological, social, and spiritual needs; or by an impulse to protest against the ineffectiveness of their conventional treatments.

Ways to evaluate unorthodox therapies were discussed, the three main criteria being: evidence for effectiveness, rationale, and consensus among informed judges. According to these criteria, there is no reason to think that cancer can be affected by any of the externally applied unorthodox remedies that are currently popular. However, a valuable sense of hope and control may derive from having something concrete that one can do, and it is also possible that certain remedies have physical effects yet to be verified. Finally, we examined some of the (mostly subconscious) reasons why those wishing to help cancer patients may advocate irrational therapies.

## Part Three

# Healing From
# Within

# 5 The Mind's Effect on the Course of Cancer

We come now to the central subject matter of this book: the idea that events in our own minds can not only influence the quality of our lives (something almost everyone would accept) but that they can affect the course of physical disease as well. In this chapter I will review evidence for an effect of mind on cancer, and in the next I discuss a scheme that may help us understand how mind (and social and spiritual events) influences bodily health.

If you have read Chapters 3 and 4, you will know that I am drawing a distinction between external treatments, a category that includes both conventional medicine and many unorthodox remedies, and internal changes aimed at healing. By internal healing, or healing from within, I mean any consciously initiated change in attitude—that is, in patterns of thought, emotion, and behavior—that helps to restore health. I do not mean to include the automatic self-repair of wounds by the body, although an effect of mental change may be to facilitate such self-repair. Obviously, there may be some overlap between external and internal healing, as when a resolution is made to seek out medical treatment or unorthodox remedies. In that case, I would classify the mental change that prompts the taking of action as "internal," and any effects of the treatment itself as "external." Internal healing may be initiated solely by the patient or, more commonly, with help from others. We will get a better sense of what the term includes in the following chapters, but for now we may note that the kinds of techniques used to heal from within are relaxation, meditation, mental imaging, awareness and change of thoughts, awareness and appropriate expression of emotions, attention to social interactions, and connecting with one's spiritual level of being.

## What is needed to begin healing from within?

Experience in our own program over nearly twenty years has taught us that by no means everybody is willing to invoke his or her own powers to assist healing.

1. *A readiness to confront the situation.* We all have a tendency to deny the seriousness of threats to life in order to allay our anxiety. This denial commonly takes the form of assuring ourselves that everything will be fine, that we don't need to worry because the medical treatment will certainly cure us. While such self-talk is comforting, it undermines motivation: without a real acknowledgment that our life is in danger we are unlikely to work at self-healing. Tragically, it is not until disease is widespread and medical options exhausted that many people turn to self-help methods. This is unfortunate because it is asking a great deal of any treatment to alter the course of advanced disease: any kind of healing, whether internal or external, has the best chance of restoring health when the disturbance is small.

2. *Open-mindedness—that is, to the view that mental change can affect the body.* More intuitive people, who have experienced for themselves their mind-body connection, are more able to adopt self-help strategies than are people who have a purely "intellectual" approach to life and the world.

3. *Willingness to work and change.* We all resist change; it is easier to maintain familiar patterns of thought and behavior, even when these are harmful. Cancer can be a fine motivator, however! Effective self-help work requires a shift in one's priorities, dropping some old habits, and making time and energy available for new activities.

4. *Help from skilled people.* While some remarkable people make substantial changes alone, most need help. I would like to re-emphasize that you need to make sure the people you choose to help you have appropriate qualifications. They should have training in psychological counseling techniques, as well as in any specific self-help methods to be taught. Usually this will mean a professional degree. Some knowledge of cancer, and experience with cancer patients, is desirable. Registration with an appropriate professional board is another important safeguard, as it means they can be held accountable for their actions; unfortunately, people without such training and accountability will often make exaggerated or harmful claims and suggestions. However, professional qualifications are no guarantee that the bearer will be helpful. And I have also met laypeople who, through their own life experiences and inner work, have gained great ability to help others heal. A good additional guiding principle is to look closely at the conduct and life of the person offering assistance: does he or she practice what is preached and exemplify the kinds of qualities you admire?

5. *Lastly, support and understanding from family and friends* is needed if anyone is going to make substantial changes in his or her life. We cast our intimate friends in particular roles, and by so doing limit their freedom. People with cancer need, first of all, the assurance of continued love and support by those around them; if they plan to adjust life patterns, permission and encouragement from others will usually be required.

## Scientific evidence for an impact of mind on health generally

My main task in this section is to review evidence for an influence of mental state on the onset and progression of cancer. But before doing that I will prepare the ground by briefly looking at two related questions: can mental change improve quality of life in cancer patients, and does the mind have an effect on diseases other than cancer?

### A. Quality of life

There are two things that we might ask of any treatment, whether internal or external: will it help us to live longer, or will the quality of our life be improved? The emphasis in studies on medical treatment of cancer has mainly been on prolonging life, without regard for its quality, although this is beginning to change. New drugs are now often evaluated not only for their effects on tumors but also for the effect they have on how the subject feels; if two different external treatment regimens have similar effects on the physical disease, the less toxic of them is obviously preferable.

There is now abundant evidence that emotional support, counseling, and coping skills like those described later can improve the quality of life of cancer patients, as measured by people's mood, social interactions, ability to work, sense of control over events, and related psychological and social indicators. For this reason alone, whether or not there is an effect on lifespan, increasing numbers of health professionals believe that psychological methods should be a part of the treatment of many serious chronic diseases, including cancer. If you have cancer, we can be confident, on the basis of research findings and clinical experience, that you will be helped emotionally by undertaking some psychological self-help. These approaches do not appeal to everyone; some patients are adequately helped by families and friends, and others prefer to cope with crises alone, usually because they have difficulty sharing their feelings or are unaware of the possible value of support from others. However, there is little doubt that quality of life can be substantially improved by efforts at healing in those individuals open to this approach; I will refer to this kind of benefit from time to time, but my emphasis will be on the more unconventional idea that the disease may be affected by internal psychological change.

## B. Evidence for effects of mind on health and disease generally

If we are going to argue that the mind can affect cancer, it is natural to put the issue in context by asking what evidence exists for its effect on other diseases. A number of observations suggest that the mind plays a dominant role in the health of those in modern Western societies. Most of this evidence relates mental state to getting sick; relatively little research has been done on the healing potential of mind.

• The most obvious influence of mind is through unhealthy behaviors. Such habits as smoking, overeating, overconsumption of alcohol and other drugs, driving carelessly, and lack of attention to needs for sleep, relaxation, and exercise are estimated to account for approximately 50 percent of premature mortality in the West. Unhealthy behaviors are particularly important as causes of cancer: as we saw in Chapter 2, approximately 85 percent of cancers could probably be avoided, notably by abolishing smoking and changing our diets.

• Certain personality traits seem to predispose people to specific diseases; the best-known example is that "type A" personalities—driven, time-anxious people who may have a lot of repressed hostility—seem more prone than others to coronary artery disease (although there is debate among experts as to exactly what the risk factors are), whereas the more relaxed "type B" individuals are less susceptible to such disease.

• People's expectations or beliefs also seem to have an important effect on their health. A number of phenomena may be grouped under this heading. In Chapter 4 I mentioned the often beneficial effects of placebos, neutral substances or procedures that are believed by the person receiving them to be effective and may cause actual physical healing of a number of symptoms or diseases. Suggestions made to those under hypnosis have also cured some physical diseases in certain circumstances, for example, long-standing skin conditions. Suggestions may also do harm, however. The phenomenon of "hex death" is well documented: a hex or spell cast on a susceptible person (typically someone who believes in such things) may bring about his or her death within a few days. It seems logical to wonder whether the mind, which has such power to cause harm, may also have a comparable ability to heal.

• Our health appears to be greatly influenced by the perception that we have a coherent support system, as is shown most dramatically by the increased death rate among men who have recently lost a spouse. Some scientists have speculated that it is important to the health of many individuals to have a sense of meaning in their lives. Recent studies have confirmed that people nearing death often demonstrate an ability to postpone their actual demise until after an important date, like a birthday or meaningful religious event.

• Related to the last section is the voluminous and often confusing research on the effects of stress on susceptibility to disease. While not all stress is "bad," and the perception of the person experiencing it is important, it has been found that people subject to a large amount of significant change in their lives over a short time are much more likely to get sick than others not so stressed.

• Evidence exists that, when information and reassurance are given to people who are about to have surgery, their healing may be faster, and time in hospital shorter, than for comparable subjects who do not get such psychological support.

• The field of psychosomatic medicine has documented the importance of mind in the development of many diseases, for example, essential hypertension, peptic ulcers, rheumatoid arthritis, and thyrotoxicosis.

• Occasional individuals have an ability to perform remarkable physiological feats, such as voluntarily controlling bleeding or pain. Biofeedback research has also demonstrated that we can learn to exert mental control over a lot of bodily functions that were previously thought to be involuntary.

• Even more basic, and probably more important than any of the above, although difficult to pin down scientifically, are the far-reaching effects of our customary modes of reacting to events around us. For example, some people see new problems as an exhilarating challenge; others see them as overwhelming or frightening, and react with what has been called "learned helplessness," a pattern that psychosomatic physicians have shown predisposes to physical disease. In poetic language we might say (as does the Buddha in the opening stanza of the Buddhist scripture the *Dhammapada*) that we mold our bodies with our thoughts. Our habitual patterns of response determine muscular tensions, which, in turn, may promote disorders of muscles (responsible for much lower back pain) and joints (possibly promoting arthritis). Thoughts are electrochemical events, taking place within nerve cells, and these chemical changes inevitably invoke parallel chemical and hormonal changes throughout the body. Thus, a constant state of vigilance or arousal, for example, activates nervous and hormonal mechanisms that raise blood pressure and contribute to heart disease. (You can read more about mind and disease generally in any of a number of popular accounts, some of which are listed in "Further Reading.")

This list of mind-disease connections reassures us that in asking if the mind can influence the course of cancer, whether to promote or retard its growth, we are not proposing something outside the realm of existing knowledge; instead we are extending the list of conditions known to be affected by mind to a disease that, for no good reason, has long been assumed by many to be largely insusceptible to such influence.

## Scientific evidence for an effect of mind on cancer

There is no single piece of evidence that would compel a skeptic to believe that mental state influences the onset or progression of cancer. However, three quite separate areas of research point to this conclusion, and, in science, such convergence is usually seen as evidence of the likely truth of an idea.

### A. Experimental studies using animals

The advantage of working with animals is that stresses can be deliberately applied or removed, in order to investigate their effects on cancer, in a way that would be unethical in humans. Many studies have shown that such stresses as shock, noise, handling, isolation, or fear may enhance tumor growth. In one example, it was found that, in a strain of mice that reliably develops mammary cancer in adult life, these tumors appeared several months earlier when the animals were subjected to environmental stress. The picture is not clear, however. Stress sometimes promotes and, in other circumstances, inhibits the development of cancer. It appears that acute stress is more likely to be a promoter of the disease in experimental animals and chronic stress a retarding influence. In one particularly interesting group of experiments, tumor-bearing mice subjected to electric shock experienced faster tumor growth than did unshocked animals. When the mice were able to avoid the shock, that is, to exert some control, the rate of tumor growth declined. And when pairs of animals received the same shock stress, but only one mouse in each pair had the ability to turn it off, the cancer grew more slowly in the mouse that had this control.[1]

Overall, experts are in agreement that there is a relationship between stress and the growth of cancers in experimental animals. This growth may be affected by the animal's ability to cope. We can also suggest some plausible mechanisms at the cellular and molecular levels (see next section). This experimental evidence increases the strength of the argument for a link between stress, coping, and cancer in humans, but does not conclusively prove it: animals obviously differ from humans in many ways, although the similarities are much more important than the differences in most biological reactions. Their cancers are, however, more often caused by viruses than are human tumors.

### B. Studies on a possible link between psychological factors ("personality") and human cancer

The idea that people with certain specific personality traits are more likely than others to contract cancer is a very old one, going back at least as far as the Greek physician Galen in the second century A.D. It is a view that has been investigated scientifically over the past thirty-five years or so—many hundreds of studies having been published during that time—but without any definite consensus being reached. There are many technical difficulties with such studies. The most obvious kind of experiment to do in this area is to assess the personalities of a group of cancer patients (in itself, a very imprecise process) and compare them with the personalities of a similar group of people who do not have cancer. Unfortunately, it is difficult to arrange for two such matched groups and yet be confident that no sources of bias have crept in, as I will discuss below. Also, such backward-looking comparisons are open to the objection that the mental characteristics of the patients may have been altered by the fact of having cancer, confusing cause and effect.

A much stronger kind of experiment involves assessing people psychologically before they get cancer, then seeing if there is any systematic difference between those subsequently contracting the disease and those who remain free from it. This is much more difficult, since we need to test very large numbers, of whom only a small proportion will get cancer later on. Alternatively, researchers have made their psychological measurements on a group of patients who already have cancer, then followed them for a period to see if those with certain kinds of personalities or coping styles do better, on average, than others. A small number of studies of this kind have been published.

One personality trait emerges fairly clearly from both of these kinds of comparisons. Research indicates that people with this trait seem somewhat more at risk of getting cancer and of doing poorly if they already have the disease. This characteristic or personality trait is a tendency to repress emotion, particularly to inhibit expression of so-called negative emotions such as anger or distress. It may evolve out of a lack of early closeness to parents. Loss of important relationships may also contribute, although the evidence for this is conflicting.

The idea that other kinds of life stress might contribute to cancer in humans, by analogy with the animal work, has been difficult to prove: again, data exist that both support and deny such an effect. Some interesting work by a group in England has shown that patients with a "helpless-hopeless" attitude to their disease were more likely to die quickly. The opposite pattern, having a "fighting spirit," was initially thought to be protective, and although very recent research has failed to confirm this, it remains a common clinical observation that people with such an attitude often seem to do better than those who feel helpless. Having good social support, less emotional distress and better coping ability have been found helpful in some studies, although again, contrary reports exist. Part of the reason for this frustrating inconsistency in results may be that the methods used to describe psychological attitudes that help people oppose cancer are almost always simple, self-report questionnaires, which do not always detect what people are really thinking and feeling.

The most dramatic examples of a possible impact of mind on human cancer are the very rare cases of "spontaneous remission," in which tumors regressed or disappeared in the absence of any medical treatment that could have been responsible. I mentioned this phenomenon in Chapter 2, and the fact that it is now generally agreed that such remissions occasionally occur. A famous example concerns a man with multiple, large lymphoid tumors who was injected with krebiozen (see Chapter 4), an ineffective alternative remedy.[2] The tumors regressed. When a newspaper report appeared, stating that krebiozen had been proved worthless, the man's tumors rapidly regrew. Physicians then injected him with what was described as "double strength" krebiozen but was, in fact, distilled water. The tumors again regressed. A further report on the uselessness of krebiozen finally convinced the patient that he had not received effective treatment, whereupon he rapidly succumbed to the disease. Such a pattern is difficult to explain except as a response of the patient's body to his mental expectations or beliefs.

Over the last twenty years I have observed a number of patients in our program who have had unexpected remissions of advanced disease that lasted for varying lengths of time. However, from such observations alone, we cannot claim that mental factors caused these regressions; other factors, not measured or controlled for, may have been responsible; we do not know how well the same people would have done without their self-help efforts. To draw conclusions about the relationship of psychological change to self-help, we need carefully done experiments with systematic observation, and an attempt to control for extraneous factors. We turn now to a brief look at work of this kind.

## C. Effects of psychological interventions on the progression of cancer

In Chapter 3 we briefly discussed "randomized controlled trials" as the most unambiguous way of testing whether or not a psychological intervention would affect average lifespan in cancer patients. You will recall that, in such experiments, a number of patients are randomly (by chance assignment) divided into two groups, which should then be approximately the same in all characteristics that might affect the course of the disease. All members of one group receive a psychological treatment program; members of the other group do not. We then ask if the group getting the intervention live longer, on average.

While results of the best-known trial of this kind were published in 1989, there has been more research of this nature since that time (and since the first edition of this book). In the earlier, well-publicized analysis by Spiegel and colleagues[3], eighty-six women with metastatic breast cancer were randomly assigned to two groups, only one of which received the psychological intervention, attendance at a weekly support group meeting for one year, plus some training in relaxation. Women receiving this intervention lived, on average, eighteen months longer than those who did not get it. This is a truly remarkable result: no drug currently exists that can prolong life reliably to this extent in women with this stage of the disease. Our own group at the Ontario Cancer Institute, Toronto has recently completed and published a similar study[4], also with patients who had metastatic breast cancer. Unfortunately, we did not find a significant impact of the psychological help on lifespan. Such contradictory results are common in trials at an early stage of testing any new procedure, including new drugs. Since both of the trials were small, it is possible that, in either or both of them, the two groups of patients were, by chance, not balanced, e.g., in the Spiegel experiment the group receiving therapy may have had less serious disease on average.

Several other less clear-cut reports of effects of psychological intervention on lifespan in cancer patients have been published in the last few years. In one of these, patients with early-stage malignant melanoma received a simple, six-session program of coping skills training. This decreased the number who had died six years later! However, by ten years, there was no significant difference between the group getting the therapy and the controls who did not. One other randomized study, designed for another purpose, showed a significant effect of a psychological intervention; two further studies, with less rigorous designs, did not find an effect. So how do we decide whether or not such therapy improves average survival? We have to wait for further experiments of the same kind; there are several now in progress in Canada and the U.S. As the work progresses, the design of the studies will improve, and we should eventually be able to tell, from the accumulating evidence whether a true effect exists, and how large it may be.

Is there another way to investigate scientifically the relationship between mental change, promoted by psychological methods (self-help or therapy), and duration of survival? In Chapter 4, while discussing "How can we evaluate remedies," I mentioned "correlative" studies, which look for a relationship between actions and consequences; this type of study can be done to relate psychological properties (attitudes and behaviors) to survival with cancer. The logic here is the same as that which we use in everyday life, i.e., in drawing conclusions about whether the things we do achieve the desired results. This kind of evidence has been used to determine that smoking causes lung cancer—the more cigarettes the greater the danger. In the field of effects of mind on cancer, there are a few studies of this kind, although most of the earlier reports were not done in a way that allowed definite conclusions. I will describe these briefly, then outline our own current program of correlative work in which we have tried to correct some of these design faults and provide more reliable results.

For many decades there have been anecdotal reports in the medical literature from physicians and psychologists who had worked with a number of cancer patients and had shown that these patients survived longer than would have been expected from the seriousness of their disease or from comparisons with national statistics. Dr. Lawrence LeShan, a psychologist, initially investigated several hundred patients and found an association between loss and susceptibility to cancer; he has written extensively about his experience,[5] from which he concludes that cancer patients need to discover, and begin pursuing, their true purpose in life (see Chapter 9). Other well-known pioneers are Dr. Carl Simonton and Stephanie Mathews-Simonton,[6] who introduced mental imaging and other psychological techniques (see Chapter 7) in complementary cancer care, and found that patients attending their clinics lived about twice as long as the recorded average for individuals with similar disease. At first sight, this finding sounds promising, but unfortunately one cannot draw strong conclusions from it because the people choosing to attend special care are in many ways different from average, being younger, more enterprising, of higher socioeconomic status, and so on. The onus is on the investigator to show that these factors do not, in themselves, account for the longer survival, independently of the intervention.

Similar caveats apply to the very interesting work of Dr. Ainslie Meares, a psychiatrist teaching intensive meditation to cancer patients, and of Dr. Bernauer Newton and colleagues, psychologists offering self-hypnosis, imaging, and related techniques; in both cases, the researchers observed an apparent relationship between their treatments and survival. Also available are accounts by individuals about their own struggles to overcome cancer, two of the best of these being the books by Claude Dosdall and Ian Gawler (see "Further Reading").

Over the last five years, at the Ontario Cancer Institute, we have done the following experiment. Twenty-two people with medically incurable metastatic cancers of various kinds were enrolled into a year of group psychological therapy. During that time, we made a detailed assessment of how "involved" they became in their psychological self-help work—how much practice they did of techniques like meditation, mental imaging, and journalizing, how dedicated they were, and how much progress they made in self-understanding and spiritual "connectedness." The twenty-two could be divided into three categories of about equal size, "highly involved," "moderately," or "slightly." There was a clear and strong relationship between living longer and being more involved with psychological self-help. In fact, two of the "highly involved" patients have had complete, five-year remissions of their disease. At the time of writing, four of the highly motivated patients are still alive, two of the moderately involved, and none of the slightly involved patients. To check that living longer was not simply the result of less serious disease we had a panel of twelve oncologists independently review the charts of each patient at the time they entered the study, and predict how long each would live. By this and other criteria (they were of similar age, and attended groups for a similar average length of time), the three categories had equally serious disease; the major difference between them appears to have been their degree of involvement in the psychological and spiritual work. However, we must note that this kind of evidence is not regarded as conclusive. Because a set of attitudes and behaviors was correlated with longer survival doesn't mean they caused it; other hidden factors could conceivably have played a role, although it is hard to see what these might have been. The most likely explanation for our results is nevertheless that dedicated self-help work prolongs life. Incidentally, the more involved people became, the better the quality of life they enjoyed also. This alone makes their efforts worthwhile.

What did the "highly involved" people do? They first appraised their situation as serious and deserving of their full effort. They were "open" or flexible enough to look at their habitual patterns and make changes (whereas people with low involvement were often preoccupied with maintaining their lives unchanged). They also believed that they could make a difference, and that psychological self-help would be effective. Driven by this strong motivation, they practiced their self-awareness, imagery, and meditation techniques regularly, often for several hours a day. For example, one of the women whose disease went into complete remission kept a journal in each of several rooms of her house so that, whenever she had an insight, she could write it down immediately! Spiritual work—trying to derive meaning from the experience and to connect with a transcendent order (Chapter 10)—was important to all of them, as were good social relationships. All of these qualities, appraisal, flexibility, motivation, dedicated action, good social and spiritual connection, seemed to go together; a person scoring high in any one of these areas was almost always high in all, and vice versa. This suggests to us that there may be a single, underlying quality responsible for healing. We will return to this in Chapters 10 and 11, but, briefly, from our research and clinical experience I would say that this quality in a person who reaches a "healed" state through his or her own efforts is a deep sense of personal authenticity or belonging, and of the intense meaningfulness of life. There is a feeling of loving all living things and of being oneself loved and worthy, accompanied by motivation to grow and evolve personally and to live life in a way that helps others. This is, of course, the kind of evolved state that spiritual traditions have been directing us towards for centuries!

## By what kinds of mechanisms could mind affect cancer?

While a detailed discussion of possible mechanisms of mind-body interaction would be too technical to be appropriate here, I want to convey that there is a growing understanding of the many cellular and biochemical pathways connecting ideas in the mind with potentially healing changes in the body. Ideas are not simply intangible, woolly things out in the ether somewhere; they are neurochemical events, taking place in the brain. A thought depends on the "firing" activity of a specific pattern of nerves, that is, on electrochemical impulses passing along and between these nerves. This activity in the brain becomes translated into events in the body through two nervous "systems." The central nervous system is the one we are all familiar with; its bodily component is the spinal cord and the nerves issuing from it. This is the "wiring" that allows us to respond to sensations like pain, and to perform the ordinary, voluntary actions of life, such as reaching for something to eat. The other, smaller system of nerves in the body, also under control of the brain, is the autonomic nervous system; its nerves go to organs other than the large muscles, and regulate such functions as digestion, excretion, respiration, and blood flow. It is called "autonomic," meaning autonomous, because for many years it was thought to be outside voluntary control; now it is known that, while the functions of this system do proceed automatically, we can change many of them through acts of will.

In addition to signals passing from brain to body by way of nerve fibers, they are also transmitted by hormones, circulating molecules that reach target organs through the bloodstream. The pituitary gland, a small structure under the brain, is the "conductor of the endocrine (hormonal) orchestra"; it receives instructions from the brain and liberates a variety of hormones, which then, in turn, activate other secretory glands, such as the thyroid and the adrenals. One of many pathways is shown in Figure 4. A product of the pituitary called adrenocorticotropic hormone stimulates the cortex, or outer part, of the adrenal glands (situated above the kidneys) to release corticosteroid or "stress" hormones, which have

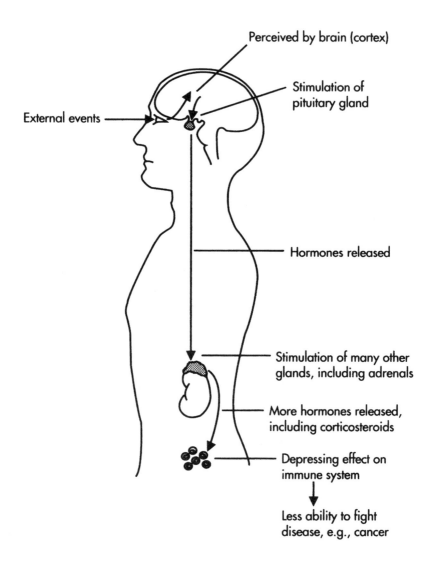

Perceived by brain (cortex)

Stimulation of
pituitary gland

External events

Hormones released

Stimulation of many other
glands, including adrenals

More hormones released,
including corticosteroids

Depressing effect on
immune system

Less ability to fight
disease, e.g., cancer

Figure 4

*One pathway through which external events, perceived as stressful, may affect our resistance to disease.*

effects on many of the body's functions in ways that may affect tumors. These molecules, together with others such as adrenaline from the inner part of the adrenals, change patterns of blood flow through the tissues, for example, reducing inflammatory reactions and influencing clotting mechanisms. Such actions can both affect primary tumors and change the likelihood of metastatic (distant) growths developing.

Figure 4 also shows one way in which the immune system (described in Chapter 2) may be affected by mental activity. For many years it was believed that this army of millions of circulating lymphocytes, and the lymph glands and other organs supporting their circulation, constituted an entirely independent system of defense, protecting the body against invasion by microorganisms without any control from the nervous or hormonal mechanisms that regulate most other functions. Now we know that this is not the case; the flourishing new scientific discipline of psychoneuroimmunology has demonstrated that mental changes, acting through neurohormonal intermediaries, can significantly influence immune responses. To the extent that the immune system protects us against tumor growth (and some reservations were expressed in Chapter 2), we now have a concrete pathway that may connect mind and cancer: mental events, including a stressful sense of lack of control, causing diminished immune activity, which in turn allows tumors to grow more readily.

## Contrasting the impact of mind on cancer with the effects of unorthodox external remedies

At this point it is instructive to compare what we have learned about the mind-cancer link with the situation that exists for unorthodox remedies applied from outside, as described in the last chapter. We discussed applying three criteria when evaluating an unconventional remedy for cancer: evidence, rationale, and consensus. We see that there is considerable convergent evidence for an impact of mind on cancer, both in experimental animals and in humans; no such evidence exists for unorthodox external remedies. There is growing understanding of the ways in which mind can influence cancer and disease generally; no comparable rationale has been presented for the external unconventional remedies. And there is a fair consensus among therapists as to what kinds of psychological help may promote healing, in contrast to the totally individualistic claims of most "alternative" therapists using external agents. For these reasons, I believe it is vital to distinguish clearly between the philosophy of helping patients mobilize their own internal resources in the struggle against disease, and the credo—we can hardly call it a philosophy—that one or another unproven and usually irrational external treatment may cure cancer.

## Why hasn't the possibility of the mind's having an impact on cancer (and other disease) influenced medical practice?

Given the converging strands of evidence supporting the idea that mental state has an impact on the course of cancer and other physical diseases, it seems odd that more attention has not been paid to using people's minds as a weapon in the struggle against illness. I think there are three main reasons for this neglect.

First, the evidence is incomplete. While the impact of the mind on certain animal cancers is undeniable, there are not enough good studies yet to convince the skeptical that mental state has a significant effect on human cancer.

Second, the evidence is scattered throughout the journals of several separate disciplines, and much of it is quite recent; thus the ideas we have been considering have generally not yet filtered down to the medical practitioner.

Third, and most important, the current theory behind medical practice sees disease as having exclusively biological causes, and treatment as being confined to externally administered agents. There is little place for mind in biomedical theory, and evidence of mental influence has to be particularly strong before it is considered at all. To many of those trained exclusively in biology or medicine, mind seems intangible. and unable to affect the concrete processes of the body. So the view that people might be able to help themselves fight disease through psychological change represents the beginning of a very fundamental shift in medical thinking. In the next chapter, I will advance a broader theory, one that takes account of all of the existing evidence and enables us to begin to understand how the higher levels of ourselves—the psychological, social, and spiritual—might be invoked to aid our healing.

## Summary

This chapter has been a brief review of the evidence for an influence of mind on disease in general and on cancer in particular. After discussing some of the prerequisites for using the mind as a tool in the struggle against disease—a willingness to confront the threat openly, to work at change, and to seek help—I listed the main areas of evidence for the overwhelming importance of mental/behavioral factors in causing disease in Western communities. Turning to the effect of mind on cancer, we found that there are three main kinds of evidence for a connection: animal experiments, studies on personality attributes (notably a tendency to repress emotion) that seem to favor cancer, and clinical trials of psychological interventions with cancer patients. We considered some of the mechanisms in the body that might connect events in the mind with cancer remission, noting the recent explosive growth of psychoneuroimmunology, a field that is documenting the influence of mind on the immune response, and hence, potentially, on cancer. Finally, the considerable evidence and plausible rationale that exist for a mind-cancer link, along with the degree of consensus among therapists, was contrasted with the lack of evidence, rationale, and consensus for the unorthodox external remedies described in Chapter 4.

# 6 | How Body, Mind, Social, and Spiritual Levels Interact

In the last chapter I discussed some of the evidence for "healing from within," that is, for the view that mental attitude or internal events or states initiated by the mind can affect the course of cancer and other diseases. We looked briefly at some of the cellular and molecular mechanisms that may translate mental events into changes in the body. In this chapter I will broaden the discussion considerably; our aim is to find a way to understand how mental, social, and spiritual changes may affect the body and thus influence health. We will end up with a theory or "model" that is very different from the kinds of explanations that are usual in biology and medicine. Instead of describing chemical or cellular processes, we will be talking in terms of the transfer of information or patterns from one "level" of the individual to another. We need this new type of theory because biomedicine (biologically based medicine), with its exclusive focus on material events, simply cannot account for the observed effect on health of many of the psychological and social factors discussed in the last chapter.

The ideas that I present here serve as a rationale for much of what cancer patients can do to help themselves. They also represent the beginnings of a theory of healing. In formulating this "model" I have drawn on a great variety of sources. For example, writers in the field of psychosomatic medicine have, since the beginning of this century, offered ways of understanding mind-body interactions. One of these is the "model" of a person as a hierarchy of different levels of organization (described below). The opinion that we need to consider *information* flow as well as material events, which is central to my scheme, has been largely overlooked by biomedicine, but is a mainstay of the philosophical field of semiotics, or theory of signs and symbols, from which we can learn a great deal that will be useful to us in understanding health in a broader context.

You will probably find that the model I propose reads like organized common sense. The conclusions I draw from it amount to a restatement, in more technical language, of ideas about healing that have been available for thousands of years, a fact that helps us have confidence in their validity. Although they are supported by the experience of many mental health professionals and of others who have worked to understand and heal themselves, they do not represent a way of looking at health and disease that has yet formed the basis for much scientific research. We have reached a cross-roads in this book: until now we have been able to draw on published scientific evidence; from this point on we will be forced to rely more on logical argument, and on a consensus from the observations and experience of many people in our own age and culture, and in other cultures at various times.

## Our many levels of organization

We are all aware that our bodies are made up of smaller building blocks; the smallest of these are the atoms and subatomic particles that combine to form larger molecules. Then, there are our cells, which combine to form tissues and organs. We sometimes see ourselves as a collection of organs, put together much like an automobile. However, unlike the car, we do not stop at our skin: in

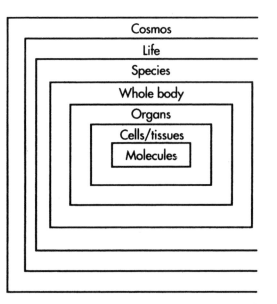

**Figure 5**
*"Map" of a person, showing some of the many structural levels. A complete line has been drawn around the "whole body" level, because we appear to be separate individuals. However, as each of us is part of higher levels, such as species, life, and the cosmos, these levels are shown as open boxes, embracing many individuals.*

order for us to stay alive there must be a constant passage of molecules from environment to body and back, most obviously during breathing, eating, and excretion, but also across the external skin itself (for example, as sweat). The digestive tract, for example, is really a tube enclosing a part of the outside world that happens to be inside us. A car would exist unchanged for a long time in outer space: a living organism could not—we depend absolutely on constant interaction with our world.

Figure 5 shows some of these levels of organization. It begins, in the center, with the familiar small components of our bodies. Continuing outwards, to bigger units, I have drawn groups of individuals as the next important "level"; we are all part of a larger social group, and could hardly live without it. We are also intimately connected with other living things and nonliving materials in our world, a fact that is becoming painfully obvious through the damage our population and technology cause the environment. Then our planet is itself a part of larger aggregations—solar system, galaxy, and universe. This kind of hierarchy has been described by many writers. If we accept that there are no real boundaries, that an individual is instead a kind of local concentration of certain materials, a pucker in the fabric as it were, Figure 5 can be seen as a "map" of a person, and each of us can be considered to contain or form part of the larger social and universal structures.

This map has two main properties. First, it describes the way in which things are organized; smaller building blocks in the middle, getting larger as we move out. It is a hierarchy, in that each level includes all of those beneath it, and the farther out we go the more complex it gets. New properties emerge as we go outwards; for example, a whole person can do things that could not be predicted from an examination of his or her component cells or organs. Second, if we disturb any level, we affect all of the others. For example, a tiny change in the DNA or genetic material of the sperm or egg can stunt an individual's growth, retard his or her intelligence, and affect a whole community. Or, in the other direction, a "high-level" change, for example, a factory shutdown, can throw people out of work, make them depressed, and cause some of them to have heart attacks or ulcers. Obviously, the changes produced in higher levels of the system by a small disturbance at a lower level, say, in a molecule or cell, may be far too insignificant to measure, but, according to physicists, this ripple effect exists nevertheless. As the Zen writers express it: "Cut a blade of grass and shake the universe!"

This view that everything is connected is hardly new; in fact, it is the central idea behind the spiritual search of many cultures, and is upheld by modern physics. We divide things up in our minds for convenience, to facilitate description and control, and in so doing lose our awareness of our intimate and necessary connection with our world.

## Where does mind fit in? Informational aspects of our being

This next section is a little more difficult because it involves looking at familiar things in a new way. However, if we are to include such concepts as "mind," "social level," and "spiritual" in our account of healing possibilities, we have to recognize that two quite different "languages" have been used to describe events affecting humans and their health—the languages of material and of information or pattern.

When we speak of "materials" we mean solid, easily measurable things like "cell," "body," and "brain." Most branches of biological science use this kind of language: we might describe a person as weighing 150 pounds, losing his hair, moving freely, and so on. Here, we are focusing mainly on the material properties of a person's state of health. "Information," by contrast, refers to any pattern in space and time; its emphasis is on the pattern itself, not on the materials displaying it. For example, "mind," an informational or pattern term, refers not to a thing, but to a (very complex) series of events and interactions; these happen to be carried out by brain cells, but many of them can also be performed by a computer. It is not the material composition of the brain that confers its unique capabilities, but its pattern of organization or structure. All objects have both material and informational aspects; we can focus our attention on either, as it suits our purpose.

Why do we need to bother with this distinction between material or substance and the pattern of its organization? The reason is that our bodies are strongly affected not only by material things but by information of many kinds. When a social event (job loss or bereavement) provokes physical illness, it is *information*, not material, that passes from one level to another of the map in Figure 5. Another example may make this clearer: If someone in the distance shouts your name, the information reaches you as a pattern of sound waves in the air, and the vibration of the eardrum is converted into neuroelectrical signals or information that flows to the brain. The brain, in turn, sends signals, via nerves and hormones, to the musculature, and you turn to face the source of the shout.

Thus, an almost purely *informational* event—the passage of a message through various levels of a person—has given rise to a large physical change, the turning of the body. There must be some material or energy to carry this information, of course, but we can readily see that this is not the important thing: if the name shouted was not your own, you would be much less likely to react, although the energy changes between the shouter and your brain would be essentially the same.

Pathological changes in the body may come about when there are repeated, arousing messages to which we cannot respond appropriately. For example, if we perceive others as hostile and untrustworthy, we will react with (usually repressed) hostility ourselves, and will be more liable, as research shows, to high blood pressure and heart disease. Or, if the messages we receive from outside are interpreted as meaning that we can't cope, we may feel helpless and hopeless. Those physicians belonging to the small specialty area known as psychosomatic medicine, who do credit the mind with power to affect health, have speculated that a helpless/hopeless orientation makes us prone to a variety of physical ailments.

This idea, that information or messages may affect our bodies, may seem obvious. After all, it is the same principle as a telephone message provoking activity, or an electronic signal guiding the movements of a machine, or the software of a computer directing the actions of the hardware. Yet this principle has been not only ignored but actively resisted by mainstream Western medicine: the mind has simply not been given credit for influencing the body. The reason has been a failure to recognize that information and material are two facets of the same events or structures; all levels of the person have both aspects, as shown in Figure 6. When I came to draw this figure for the first time, some years ago, I got quite a surprise: we don't even have the words to describe the informational correlates of some of the structures on the map! "Mind" is an informational or pattern term corresponding roughly to "brain" (although other parts of the body also contribute to it), and "social order," although a clumsy expression, denotes the patterns of

**Material Structures**    **Informational Terms**

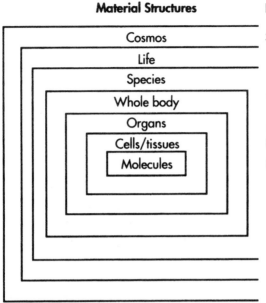

| Material Structures | Informational Terms |
|---|---|
| Cosmos | Spiritual/existential order |
| Life | Biosphere, ecosystem |
| Species | Social order |
| Whole body | } Mind |
| Organs | |
| Cells/tissues | Lymphocytes — immune system |
| Molecules | DNA — genetic code |

Figure 6

*The "structural map" of an individual that follows from Figure 5. On the right-hand side I have added "informational" terms (see text) that correspond to different levels of structure. Thus, "mind" is an informational or pattern term corresponding (approximately) to brain, and "genetic code" describes the informational content of DNA.*

relations within groups of people. But what corresponds to "organ" or "molecules"? There is no general term, so I've given some specific examples. And the best I could do for a term describing the pattern aspect of the natural world as a whole was "ecosystem" or "biosphere." The correspondence between "cosmos" and "spiritual order" is simply a way of thinking about the spiritual as a property emerging from the total organization of the universe, much as mind can be thought of as emerging from brain. These are undoubtedly oversimplifications, aids to thought really. Mind and spirit are probably much more than this, and perhaps have non-material aspects that we simply can't fit into a model like Figure 6.

How is all this important for healing? Each of us has many levels (see Figure 5). When we change one, we unavoidably change them all, to at least some degree. When any change takes place, at any level, both the material structure and the pattern of organization or information in that structure are changed together: material and the pattern of its arrangement are two necessary properties of any object or event (Figure 6). Changes in pattern/information therefore provoke changes in material, and we observe that information or messages, from within and without, have a powerful influence on the state of our bodies.

The failure of biomedicine to credit information with the power to change the body has resulted in a medical system that concentrates almost entirely on the material; the only way to treat a tumor is to cut it out, irradiate it, or poison it! Yet we know that messages can affect health—the evidence is all around us. An idea or attitude is both an informational and a physical/material event, involving chemical and electrical changes in the brain and elsewhere. An idea can affect our bodies as profoundly as a direct physical assault (consider an unexpected telephone call saying that a member of the family has just been killed in a traffic accident). The rationale behind the kinds of adjunctive, self-initiated treatments for physical disease advocated in this book, and behind much "traditional" healing, is that messages or information within the mind and coming from any of our higher levels may significantly affect the health of the body.

## The need for change, to affect cancer

Some ill health seems to be largely caused by external agents, such as accidents or infectious organisms. Much of it, however, including most of those diseases currently important in Western society such as heart disease and cancer, occurs because of conditions that develop within the body over a long period of time. In Chapter 2 we discussed the likelihood that potentially cancerous cells are being generated all the time but are usually restrained from growing into clinical cancer by the body's normal control mechanisms. This leads us to a very important practical conclusion: we may reasonably expect to change the rate of growth of a cancer by changing the conditions surrounding it in the body. A cancer has, in a sense, "learned" to grow under the conditions in which it finds itself. It has evolved, generating further new variants, some of which are able to grow faster under the prevailing conditions than others. Our strategy, then, is to so change the state of the body that it will become difficult or impossible for the cancer to continue to grow. That this is realistic is shown by evidence briefly referred to in Chapter 2; when either human or animal tissues are searched systematically, "covert" or "dormant" cancers are found that remain quiescent for years. Also, after removal of a primary breast cancer, a person may be apparently free of disease for twenty years or more, then suddenly experience a "shower" of metastases. It seems almost certain that this happens because of a change in conditions in the body, and highly probable that mental or social events may contribute to such changes.

I have pointed out that most medical intervention in the West is external, the patient being regarded as passive. By contrast, a patient actively involved in healing will be initiating changes internally. You might think of those changes as an attempt to readjust regulatory processes from within, an "internal chemotherapy," albeit of a benign and nontoxic kind.

The mind of the person with disease is the prime mover in this readjustment. If you should doubt its power, recall the evidence reviewed in Chapter 5 for the mind's having an effect on cancer, and on disease generally. Consider also how different you feel when you are "up" from when you are depressed. Such different feelings reflect large differences in actual physiology: brain-wave patterns vary with mood state and thought processes, as can be shown with sophisticated modern scanning instruments; heart rate and patterns of blood flow around the body are greatly affected by ideas and moods; breathing patterns are profoundly changed by mood— contrast the way we hold our breath, or take rapid, shallow breaths when we are afraid, with the slow, deep breaths of the relaxed state; more detailed adjustments occur in the circulation of cells and molecules in different mental states, for example, corticosteroids (stress hormones) in the blood will cause certain immune cells to be removed from circulation. It is therefore reasonable to propose that mental state may affect the suitability of the internal environment for cancer growth, as we have argued before.

What practical recommendations follow from this? We have to admit that not enough is known about the connection between mental state and cancer growth to make specific, detailed recommendations. Research on such questions, and on the whole approach of using *information* as a tool for affecting physiology, is in its infancy. It is also probable that the most favorable mental state varies somewhat from one person to another, and for different types of cancer. Obviously, the answers to these questions will be complex. However, we can make a reasonable assumption: trying to promote the best overall state of balance within the body should best oppose the progress of any disease, including cancer.

What does "state of balance" mean? It sounds like a tautology, to say that cancer is best fought by promoting balance or health. I am going to try to make this recommendation more concrete by reintroducing the concept of "connectedness." I have used the term before, but we can return to it with more understanding now after our discussion on the informational or pattern aspects of events in the body. "Connectedness" means free flow of information between the various levels of the person, including the mental, social, and spiritual. What I propose is that health depends on optimal connectedness, not necessarily on the maximum amount of information flow—too much stimulation can be as harmful as too little—but on a continual buffering passage of messages from one level to another.

## Is there any evidence for the healing power of connectedness?

The healing power of connectedness has not been directly tested by modern biomedicine, which does not yet think in those terms. However, the concept appears in various forms in the work of many therapists and in many cultures. Historically, balance, harmony, and wholeness have been seen as almost synonymous with health; in fact, our word *healing* comes from the Old English *haelen*, to make whole. Theorists in psychosomatic medicine have repeatedly pointed out that mental and social events affect physical health, as in, for example, the influential biopsychosocial model proposed by psychiatrist George Engel.[1] Pioneers in the cancer/healing field, such as Lawrence LeShan,[2] have stressed the importance for cancer patients of finding out what they are really meant to do with their lives, advocating, in other words, connection with an authentic life purpose. (I will have more to say about this later.) A.M. De la Pena has written a brilliant, but neglected, work,[3] arguing that cancer is specifically promoted by too much or too little information flow between parts of the organism.

One way of testing the validity of the relationship between connectedness and healing is to ask if its opposite, separation between parts and levels of a person, promotes disease. At the level of the tissues, it is evident that connection to blood flow and nerves is essential for health. Some intriguing research demonstrates that if a plastic sheet is inserted into tissues, tumors tend to develop on both sides of the sheet; this effect seems to be caused by the interruption of communication rather than by the material itself, since such tumors do not develop if small holes are first made in the plastic sheet! At the mental level, an inadequate awareness of unconscious drives may lead to neurotic thoughts and behaviors. In social terms, we have seen that health is promoted by adequate support from others; bereavement, for example, may make us liable to disease. And healing at the spiritual level is an attempt to diminish the separation between the individual and a Higher Power or God.

It may seem like mere common sense to propose that healing should go along with connectedness. We are familiar with the concept in many aspects of our lives—families, organizations, cities, nations, all run better with good lines of communication. The "natural" state of an individual would appear to be one in which free communication takes place among his or her various parts, and between self and others. However, we must be aware that we are relying on intuition and analogy here: the notion has not been scientifically tested.

Our basic approach in subsequent chapters will be to find ways to foster connectedness, or wholeness, within ourselves, taking the self to include the higher levels I have described. To this we will add attempts to influence physical and mental processes specifically with the use of imagery and self-suggestion.

## Healing as a journey

By now it will be very clear that I am not advocating any simple alternative solutions, such as dietary additives or psychological tricks, to the problem of having cancer. Instead, I am proposing a process, a journey, with the aim of recovering connections to all parts of ourselves. This process clearly requires effort, time, and change; the learning of new skills; the alteration of perceptions about oneself and the world. Ultimately, it is a journey of self-discovery, the path of the hero, as recognized in many cultures, and beautifully described by Joseph Campbell.[4] Healing and understanding are closely allied; in the broadest meaning of the word, healing becomes this understanding and experiencing of the relationship between all aspects of ourselves, and between ourselves and what we have learned to call the outside world. So my thesis is in no way original, but is simply a particular example of the evolution of the individual toward identity with something larger, although in this case undertaken in the hope of physical cure. The disease becomes the stimulus, and the response of the exceptional patient is a search for meaning or wholeness, a theme to which we will return.

## Summary

An individual has many "levels": atoms, molecules, cells, and organs, and also forms part of the social and global spheres. These levels are not separate from one another: each of us is continuous with our environment. I have described the world as a giant structure, of which each of us forms a part. When any change occurs in any part of this structure, corresponding alterations occur at all levels: our bodies are thus affected, not only by biochemical events but also by the social and ecological dimensions.

To this awareness we added a second set of ideas—that there are two separate kinds of language needed to describe any natural event: the familiar language of material and that of information or pattern. The second refers to the way material is organized; "mind," "social order," and "spiritual" are examples of terms that are informational, and not primarily about material or physical things. Biomedicine has, by and large, failed to make this distinction, and to recognize that information, in this sense, has a vital and often predominant influence on health and disease.

I then argued that *change* in the internal milieu of the body is necessary to provide conditions unfavorable to the continued growth of cancer, and that useful change may be brought about, not only by external treatments but by alterations initiated from within, by the mind. An idea or attitude has both informational content and a physical basis: by manipulating information we change the underlying physical structure. At the present state of knowledge, the most useful type of change seems to be fostering "connectedness," or the free flow of information between all parts and levels of the person. Thus healing becomes a journey of self-discovery, the recovery of connections between all aspects of ourselves.

# Strategies of Self-initiated Healing

Let us assume that we accept the possibility of helping ourselves against cancer by making changes that begin in the mind. The question we come to now is the practical one: "What should I do?"

In this chapter, and the next three, I will lay out the strategy of self-help that follows from an attempt to become more connected with all aspects of ourselves. My hope is to give you an overview of what is possible, a road map of the journey, touching on a variety of therapies and how they contribute to the overall aim. With this as background you will be better equipped to seek the specific help and instruction you need to assist your own healing. This strategy of fostering connectedness, as should be clear by now, is not arbitrary, but is based on quite a large body of experience and theory. The theoretical background was sketched out in Chapter 6. The experience comes not only from our programs for patients at the Ontario Cancer Institute, and my own struggles with cancer, but from books, papers, workshops, and discussions with many therapists, principally in North America, who have been teaching adjunctive mental techniques to cancer patients for many years. I have found it very reassuring that there is a high level of agreement among these professionals as to what is helpful; their reaction to the idea of connectedness is usually: "Of course." However, we have to remember that, as yet, little research has been done that specifically tests a relationship between connectedness and physical health. It is certainly not a mainstream idea, and by no means all those with training in the mental health fields would subscribe to the philosophy of this book (although they are much more likely to do so than are professionals without psychological training).

In our subsequent descriptions we are thus drawing on the impressions of a selected group of health care workers, and on subjective experience, not on scientific data. I believe it is reasonable to assert that the overall strategy is health-promoting, but that the details of how best to help people in this way are by no means entirely clear as yet.

### Stages in the healing journey

I have found that the self-help work many people do can be arranged into three main phases that represent stages of the healing journey. These phases may overlap in time, and some individuals don't get past the first one, but for those who persist, all three are usually recognizable. The first is "taking control," learning what can be done to have some control over the way in which we react, mentally and physically, to our environment. The second phase I call "getting connected," to signify that the process of self-understanding has now become of value in and for itself. The third may be termed the "search for meaning"; it seems to evolve naturally from a growing realization that we are not entirely separate entities, but are part of a larger social, natural, and spiritual world.

The underlying idea behind the stage of taking control is that we can become much more aware than we usually are of how we react to ideas or to external stimuli, and can use this awareness to change our thoughts and behaviors. In our program, we begin our courses with a discussion of stress management, something that most people see as having relevance to themselves. Various methods of deep relaxation are among the first techniques usually taught in self-control courses: they release muscle tension, thus counteracting some of the effects of stress, and provide an initial demonstration of the way our minds affect our bodies. The next step is to learn to watch our minds more closely, to interrupt the flow of critical and negative ideas, replacing them, at least some of the time, with more optimistic thoughts.

Mental imaging, for example, picturing our defenses overcoming the cancer, has been advocated by many therapists as a way of trying to influence bodily processes through the mind. It also helps us feel more in control. Learning to acknowledge and appropriately express our emotions is also an important means of changing how we feel. This growing awareness of thoughts and feelings can be applied in the social sphere, helping us to interact in a more satisfying way with friends and family, and it can be used to make changes in lifestyle and to clarify goals. A strong "fighting spirit" or will to live helps people combat their cancer, and the techniques I have just described can strengthen such an attitude. Many people decide that learning these techniques of "taking control" is as much as they wish to do.

Those who become very involved in learning to help themselves move on to the second stage, "getting connected." It is a broader based, more mature perspective; while control is still sought, the emphasis is more on understanding ourselves. Thus the habit of watching our minds leads to keeping a psychological journal, in which significant emotional events are recorded and analyzed. Often, people exploring at this level go into psychotherapy to assist them in understanding normally subconscious thought processes. Some people begin to use mental imaging for purposes other than relaxation or dictating to the body, for example, "visiting" and "consulting with" an "Inner Healer" (in the imagination), and working on relationships by imagining the desired changes. Meditation techniques are central to this stage, and can not only convey some of the same benefits as relaxation but also allow the beginning or strengthening of connection to a spiritual order. This work leads to a realization that we largely create our own worlds, and that we are connected to everything, in the sense that everything we do and all that happens apparently "outside" us has an impact on our minds and bodies.

As this discovery of connectedness continues, it often evolves into a search for meaning in one's existence. This is not the distant philosophical concept that it may first appear: meaning comes from *relationship*—of all aspects of ourselves, one to the other (for example, body to mind and spirit), and of ourselves to other people and events. A central technique in this search for meaning is reviewing one's life history, which helps us to see what patterns have been repeated and how apparently distinct events may be related. It also helps clarify what is important for the future. Strange though it may sound, a sense of meaning may often be found in the cancer itself, via such techniques as an imaginary trip into the region of the body affected by it. In this phase, social connectedness becomes a higher priority, and may displace earlier, more impersonal goals. Spiritual connectedness takes on new importance, particularly to people whose lives are threatened, and it can be strengthened with different forms of meditation, reading of classical scriptural works or expositions, reflection, prayer, meeting with others for this common purpose, and cultivating an openness to a larger unity, in whatever way this is understood.

## Using the idea of "levels" to organize our efforts

Paradoxically, the person who decides to help him- or herself faces such an abundance of ideas in the form of popular books, articles, and media presentations that it is easy to become confused. Much of this information is about diet or other "external" remedies, which can be evaluated critically according to the criteria outlined in Chapter 4. But a great deal of information and a wide array of therapeutic techniques are also available for helping ourselves from within. It can be helpful to have some scheme or system within which to place the various approaches. The "levels" model is a very useful one for this purpose. I think you will find that most of

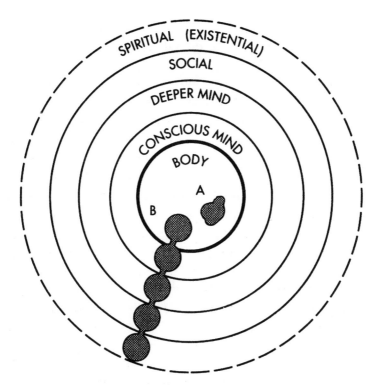

**Figure 7**

*The main levels or properties of a person with which we can work to restore health.*

*A = disease according to the biomedical view (i.e., restricted to the body)*

*B = disease, on a broader, multilevel view (i.e., affecting all levels or properties of a person, and susceptible to influence at all these levels)*

the therapies you hear about fit within the overall idea of becoming more connected with all levels of ourselves.

Figure 7 is a simplified version of the figures in Chapter 6. It shows five main levels of the person: body, conscious mind, "deeper mind" (which is meant to include emotions, plus ideas and fantasies not normally in awareness), social, and spiritual or existential. I have mixed material and informational terms (discussed in Chapter 6) in creating this map: for practical purposes, this mix is appropriate. I will discuss later the different techniques that may be used to promote connectedness to each of these parts of ourselves. However, it should be noted here that most therapists work

## Table 1

*Strategies of self-initiated healing (healing from within). The three main stages of self-help work are shown across the top of the table: "taking control," "getting connected" and "finding meaning." The five main levels or aspects of the person at which self-healing work may be done are listed down the left side.*

|  | Taking Control |
| --- | --- |
| Underlying themes | Awareness of mind-body connection can be greatly increased. We can make a difference to what happens in our bodies. |
| 1. Body | Looking after body: diet, exercise, rest. Deep-relaxation techniques. |
| 2. Conscious mind | Awareness and control of thoughts. Fun/play. Positive affirmations/will. |
| 3. Deeper mind | Awareness and appropriate expression of emotions. Mental imagery of healing. |
| 4. Social | Good communication. Reaching out and allowing support. Purposeful activity/work/creativity. |
| 5. Spiritual (Existential) | Beginning awareness of spiritual being. Reading. Mind quietening. Prayer. |
| Approaches that involve all levels | Stress control. Clarifying goals. Lifestyle change. |
| Implications | Responsibility? Blame and guilt? Empowerment. Improvement in mood and quality of life. Hope. |

| Getting Connected | Finding Meaning |
|---|---|
| We largely construct our worlds. We need to experience our connection to everything. | All events have meaning/relationship. |
| Becoming more aware of mind-body connections. Techniques like yoga, t'ai chi. | Finding meaning in body events (muscle, tension, symptoms, disease). Body as a vehicle. |
| Becoming an observer of our own thoughts. Keeping a psychological journal. Psychotherapy: understanding our defenses. | Observing and dropping (some of) our mental constructions. Quiet mind/mantra. Finding meaning in events at nonmaterial levels. |
| Awareness of connections between thoughts and emotions. Psychotherapy. Imagery for wider purposes, e.g., dropping resentments, setting goals, self-concept. | Dialogue with "Inner Healer," and with the cancer. Dream analysis. Less driven by emotional reactions. |
| Feeling and expressing love for others (working on our relationships). Altruism. | Less dependency on other people. Unconditional love. Selfless service to others. |
| Mind-quietening: meditation, prayer. Orienting life toward spiritual connectedness. Reading. Meeting with others for spiritual practice. | Ego surrender/nonattachment. Trust. Being a "channel" for higher-order purpose. |
| Journal-keeping, psychotherapy, support. | Writing a life story. Consulting "inner wisdom." Using "light." "Letting go" of personal control. |
| We are part of a larger whole. | We discover meaning and purpose through integration with a larger order. |

at some of these levels and do not address others. Thus most psychologists, and psychiatrists who do psychotherapy, will deal with events at the psychological and social levels, but may not be highly sensitive to mind-body connections or to the spiritual dimension. Within their specific areas of interest, individual professionals tend to specialize in particular approaches, acquiring more expertise in those than in others. In the program with which I am involved we try to cover the whole range, but in so doing have to sacrifice some of the sophistication that specialization allows.

Note that I have divided up the terrain of self-help strategies into three stages (control, connectedness, and meaning) and five levels of work (body, conscious mind, deeper mind, social, and spiritual), making fifteen categories in all. In Table 1 I list the main concepts and techniques associated with each of these categories. These divisions are designed to make a mass of material more comprehensible. I feel a bit embarrassed about doing this after having just argued that there are no real divisions between the different parts of ourselves! However, it seems that we cope better with ideas that are laid out in some sort of order.

In the next sections we will examine some of the demands self-help makes on those practicing it, and explore criticisms of the approach offered by some professionals. In the following three chapters I will go through the material in Table I in more detail.

## The role of the will in self-help

Whether or not people undertake to try to help themselves against disease, and to what lengths they are prepared to go, depends on a complex mixture of motivation, beliefs, and psychological barriers. Figure 8 shows some of the main decision points along the path to healing: this is a personal view, based on my clinical and introspective experience.

The first decision is whether to attempt self-help beyond presenting oneself for medical treatment. Most people currently do not—largely, I think, because of societal ignorance of what is possible, and the muddying of the waters by extremist claims, which understandably discourage some individuals (including many physicians) from considering self-help seriously. For the minority who do decide to see what they can accomplish for themselves, and who find reliable assistance, there are still many obstacles to be overcome. The first requirement is some belief that mental efforts can indeed make a physical difference: the more materialistic one's outlook, the more difficult this is to accept. If the person can remain open-minded enough to learn techniques like relaxation and meditation, and practice them for a while so that benefits are felt, any skepticism may be allayed. Then there needs to be a genuine, strong desire to live, which also implies some sense of purpose. Nobody wants to suffer, and few are aware of any desire to die prematurely, but it is not at all uncommon to find that, under the surface, there is a lack of enthusiasm for life, or a wish to escape from a demoralizing situation (such as an unhappy marriage), which undermines the struggle to survive. I vividly remember a young mother who told me her immediate reaction to the diagnosis of cancer was: "Thank goodness. Now I can leave my job!" Such attitudes may obviously undermine the struggle to survive. In Figure 8 I have shown these attitudes and others as blind alleys inhibiting further progress.

Given belief and motivation there is still a continuing struggle to do the work needed if you are to understand yourself and make changes. This is true of all good psychotherapy: it is not that the process is unrelieved drudgery—often it is exhilarating and intensely rewarding for its own sake—but we all seem to get stuck in ruts of behavior and thinking from which it is very difficult to budge us. We are afraid to change. Often the obstacles are unconscious and unrecognized, and ill health can sap the strongest motivation. In order to keep going beyond the first few months, it is necessary that the process become interesting and worthwhile for its own sake. It is rather like maintaining an exercise program: we need the reward of feeling good as we do it, and not simply a vague long-term goal of keeping fit. Finally, and this may not apply to everyone, I think people need to find compelling, stimulating

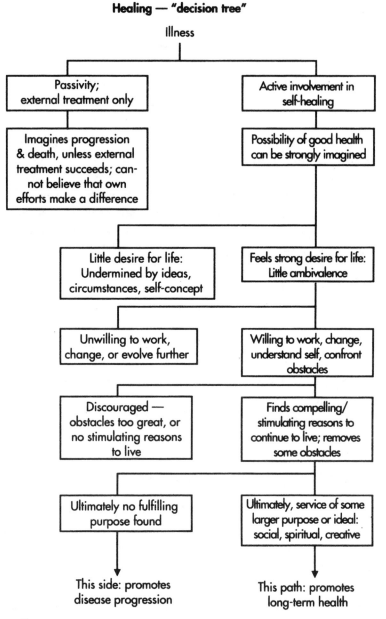

**Healing — "decision tree"**

Illness

| Passivity; external treatment only | Active involvement in self-healing |
|---|---|
| Imagines progression & death, unless external treatment succeeds; cannot believe that own efforts make a difference | Possibility of good health can be strongly imagined |
| Little desire for life: Undermined by ideas, circumstances, self-concept | Feels strong desire for life: Little ambivalence |
| Unwilling to work, change, or evolve further | Willing to work, change, understand self, confront obstacles |
| Discouraged — obstacles too great, or no stimulating reasons to live | Finds compelling/ stimulating reasons to continue to live; removes some obstacles |
| Ultimately no fulfilling purpose found | Ultimately, service of some larger purpose or ideal: social, spiritual, creative |

This side: promotes disease progression

This path: promotes long-term health

Figure 8

*A healing "decision tree." At all nodal points, the person wishing to be actively involved in his or her own healing is confronted with a choice: that on the right side may promote healing, whereas that on the left hinders it.*

goals over and above physical health, preferably an involvement with some purpose beyond their own well-being. Victor Frankl makes this plain in his book about survivors of concentration camps, who kept themselves going by focusing on such goals as returning to their loved ones.[1] An ambition to help others with the insights we gain through work on ourselves can also be a strong motivator.

Very few people manage to travel all the way along this path. Some are felled by overwhelming disease; many drop out early because they cannot bring themselves to make the necessary changes in their lives, even when they are apparently convinced that these changes would help them. So, at present, the full healing journey is undertaken by very few. I am no longer surprised or particularly discouraged by this fact. Our materialistic society provides little inducement to its members to attempt this kind of personal transformation, and I have learned how difficult it is to make changes in myself. However, if we can establish, by scientific experiment, that there is a relationship between connectedness and physical healing, and if this kind of help then becomes part of the health care routinely offered to cancer patients and others, the journey should become more appealing to much greater numbers of people.

## Implications of taking some responsibility for self-healing

If people come to believe that they can make a difference to their disease through their own efforts, what happens if they don't try, or if they do try to help themselves but the cancer is unaffected? Will they not feel guilty, or see themselves as "failures"? Is advising cancer patients to help themselves a kind of victimization of the needy? And will some people abandon medical treatment in favor of "unproven" remedies? These questions reflect the criticisms that have been leveled by conservative critics against the philosophy of adjunctive self-help that I am advocating in this book. They are serious concerns, and must be addressed.

It is clear that the weight given to these criticisms depends on whether we believe there is any evidence that changes in attitude and behavior can make a difference to disease progression. If we believe that such changes make absolutely no difference—a view still commonly held by many medical practitioners—then the only benefit of self-help could be temporary optimism, often labeled "false hope." The adjective indicates that there is held to be no real basis for the hope, and it is often implied that, in the end, the patient's disillusionment more than cancels out any temporary psychological benefits. In response, I would say that it is true that patients are often devastated when cancer progresses, but "false" hope may be engendered by medical treatment as well as by other efforts to heal. I also share the contempt most professionals feel for therapists who make strong claims for any kind of healing agent or procedure that is not backed by some evidence, and worse, for those who exploit needy people for profit. However, hope itself is always uplifting for the patient, and it is not clear that subsequent disappointment always outweighs its benefits.

As to whether a belief in the possibility of helping oneself is justified, I hope readers have seen by now that there is considerable evidence for it; undoubtedly, the quality of life can be improved, and, very probably, the progression of disease slowed in at least some cases. So, the hope that we may help ourselves, at least to some degree, is not unfounded. On the contrary, those practitioners who, without knowing the evidence, dogmatically assert to patients that they cannot make a difference by their own efforts may themselves be doing a great deal of harm, both by discouraging self-help attempts and by inhibiting people from having some legitimate optimism.

A more tangible objection than false hope is the fear that patients will abandon potentially helpful medical treatment in favor of ineffective alternatives. This concern is justified in those situations where the medical treatment does have a significant probability of curing or alleviating the disease, and the alternative does not. As I mentioned earlier, in my experience, and as Dr. Cassileth's survey showed,[2] such unwise choices are made, but rarely. There seems no reason for complaint, however, when cancer is advanced and a patient decides to stop a toxic regimen that is given virtually no chance of having significant effects, and instead tries some alternative, less unpleasant remedy, or indeed, abandons all treatment.

To what extent are we "responsible" for our illnesses? This seems to depend very much on our awareness. For example, it is now clear, as it was not forty years ago, that smoking increases the risk of lung cancer, and most would agree that those who continue to smoke, knowing the risks, bear some responsibility for any ill health that results. At present, the possibility that lifestyle and thought-style contribute to the progression of existing cancer is much less clear, but extreme opinions in either direction—the view that the patient can do nothing with his or her own mind, or, conversely, that the patient can totally determine outcome if only he or she tries hard enough—seem equally unwarranted.

Responsibility is a word that needs to be used carefully: it includes both the idea of "liability," which leads to guilt and is harmful, and the idea of "agency," or ability to act, which leads to self-help and is useful. There is certainly no reason for guilt if we promoted disease without being aware that it was the consequence of what we were doing, and, once disease exists, there is little point in dwelling on whether or not we may have contributed to it by our thoughts and actions, except to the extent that changing them may make a difference now. We can, however, take some responsibility for what happens to us once we have a disease, including seeking the best possible medical care, and also doing everything else that we understand may help us. Stephen Levine, who has written some excellent books on responding to life-threatening illness (see "Further Reading"), talks of being responsible *to* our disease, not *for* it; this seems to me to encourage action without promoting guilt.

In the classes offered as part of our program we use the model of a balance of forces (Figure 9). On one side of the fulcrum is a big weight, the cancer, which tries to bring down its host. On the

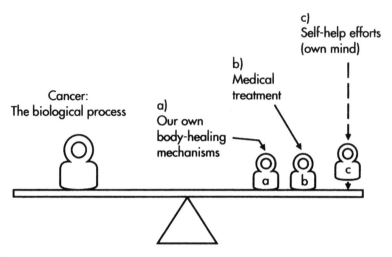

Figure 9

*Health and disease as a balance of forces or weights. The biological progression of cancer may be opposed by the three forces shown on the right side.*

other side are collaborative but smaller weights: the person's immune and other defense systems, medical treatment, and an optional third weight, his or her self-help efforts. These may or may not be enough to tip the balance toward health; their ability to do so depends on a lot of factors, in particular on how "heavy" the cancer is. But if the disease progresses in spite of individual effort, there is no cause for recrimination. We simply do not know the relative sizes of these weights, and whether any feasible form of self-help can make a difference to the growth of the cancer. Clearly, the more advanced it is, and the faster it is growing, the more difficult it will be to influence its progress by any means, medical or otherwise.

It is really rather surprising that, in a society like ours, where individual initiative is so highly prized in most fields, the possibility that individuals can influence the course of their diseases has been so little explored. This climate of incomprehension prevents people from trying to help themselves. The realization that our own actions and thoughts may make a difference can be a daunting one; that is why this book has been written. But it is also a realization that allows us to respond to crisis authentically, as human beings, not as helpless animals.

## Summary

We have outlined a strategy for self-initiated healing based on the aim of increasing the connectedness between all parts or levels of ourselves. The healing journey has three main stages: learning to take some control; becoming involved in a deeper understanding of ourselves as an end in itself; and shifting to a search for meaning, rather than comfort only, as a central focus in life. We discussed some of the decisions that need to be taken along this healing journey, and considered the main objections that are sometimes raised to the philosophy of self-help in healing. Our conclusion was that it is possible, and important, that we learn to take some responsibility for our health at all stages when we have the power of choice, and that we can do this without fostering guilt or a sense of failure if the disease progresses.

# 8 | Taking Control

In this chapter, and in the two that follow, we will discuss the principles behind the main approaches for helping oneself toward optimal health at all levels (as outlined in Table 1, on pages 106–107). The levels idea, as pointed out earlier, is somewhat artificial—any event at one of them affects the rest—but it is a useful device for organizing our discussion. Similarly, the process of "taking control" overlaps with "getting connected" (the subject of the next chapter), but isolating each of them helps us to lay out our healing journey.

The main aim of the early stages of all self-help work is to become more aware of how our minds and bodies react to external events, and to learn some control over these reactions. Most of us start with very little such awareness, a fact that becomes evident only as we learn to increase it. Awareness must precede attempts to control, otherwise we don't know what changes we need to make; for example, we can't relax deeply without recognizing the signs of muscle tension, and we can't genuinely express love toward others without first identifying the other ideas and feelings that interfere with this expression. Having acknowledged our current mental and physical activities, we then have the choice of dropping some of them (a process that is almost always valuable in itself) and replacing them with others more likely to promote health. We come to realize that much of what happens to us internally is determined by our own ideas and perceptions, that the events outside are simply triggers, and that, to a large extent, we create our own internal state by the constant flow of ideas and criticisms that passes through our minds.

## Body: level 1

Living things are never still. Apart from the constant breathing, blood flow, digestion, and other processes, we are reacting to environmental changes all the time, even in sleep. The purpose of this constant adjustment is to promote our survival. Because of our large brains and developed culture, we humans, unlike other animals, can become aware of this adjustment process, and can modify it when it is not functioning for our benefit.

An excellent way to begin self-help instruction is with a consideration of stress, something almost everyone is aware of by now. As Figure 10 shows, "stress" is a process, or pathway For example, a sudden frightening event (the "stressor"), such as a car screeching to a stop near us as we cross the road, may lead to a perception of danger in our minds and to a feeling of fear. Immediately, changes occur in the body: muscles tense, adrenaline is released, heart and breathing rates go up, and the body is ready for rapid self-protective action. Such dramatic threats may happen only occasionally, but our lives are full of smaller challenges and frustrations: the lineup at the checkout counter, the family member who interferes with our plans, the postage stamp we can't find when we need it, the noise from an adjacent apartment. And there are insidious stressors lurking within: perhaps a sense that we are not adequate to perform some necessary task or that our daily round has lost its savor, or that life itself is threatened by disease. We tend to react to all of these events and perceptions with a primitive "fight-or-flight"

| The stress pathway ——> disease | What we can do to help ourselves |
| --- | --- |
| (1) Events outside of ourselves (stressors), e.g., problems, responsibilities, threats | ◄—— Reduce our exposure to these conditions. Lifestyle change |
| (2) Perception by the mind, e.g., labeling events as difficult or threatening | ◄—— Change how we label things, e.g., "disasters" become "inconveniences" |
| (3) Our mind reacts: ready for "fight or flight." Feels fear, aggression, helplessness | ◄—— Reduce mental reactions: relaxation, positive self-talk |
| (4) Physical stress reaction: The body becomes aroused, e.g., heart rate rises, breathing gets shallow and fast, sweating begins, muscles tense | ◄—— Relax, focus on positive thoughts and images, exercise, humor, talking, tranquilizing drugs |
| (5) Chronic discomfort and disease: headaches, gastrointestinal upsets, hypertension, anxiety and depression, etc. | ◄—— Work with self-help techniques. Seek medical help |

Figure 10
*The "stress pathway," and how we can help ourselves avoid stress reactions.*

reaction, which may have been appropriate for our forbears, but is seldom useful for modern humans. As a result, we are constantly being dragged away from the relatively calm, balanced state most conducive to heating. While some stimulation is necessary for health, modern city dwellers are often so bombarded with stimuli that they live in a perpetual state of overreaction.

Constant stress leads to various kinds of disease. This connection has been quite well documented, although for cancer it is not as clear as for other conditions. As Figure 10 shows, we can interrupt the stress pathway at several points: avoiding unnecessary stressors (for example, unwanted social functions, violent TV shows); changing how we label events (an irritating colleague might become a "needy person" rather than an "obnoxious pest"); and learning to relax an already tense body, with standard techniques.

There are a number of well-researched techniques for relaxing body and mind. In general, the process is one of quieting and focusing the mind, and identifying and letting go of excessive tension in the main muscle groups. The student either sits comfortably or lies down, and receives a series of instructions (initially from an audiotape or a therapist, although later the subject can direct his or her own relaxation). Typically, the first of these instructions may be to pay attention to the breathing, not letting the mind wander; then focusing on different muscles in turn, sometimes tensing them deliberately at first, to exaggerate the discomfort and make it recognizable, then letting it go. The exercise may end with the subject imagining an internal "room" or beautiful scene; dwelling on such imagery often enhances the relaxation, and may be used as a relaxation technique in its own right.

This deliberate, focused relaxation process produces an effect that feels quite different from the more familiar ways of relaxing, such as interacting socially, listening to music, reading, or watching TV. Herbert Benson, one of the pioneering researchers in this area, calls it "the relaxation response."[1] It is associated with some definite physiological changes, for example, slower breathing and heart rate, reduced blood pressure, decreased muscular tension, and different patterns of electrical activity in the brain. These changes are the opposite of those experienced under stress.

Many other methods exist that promote deep relaxation. Simply sitting with the eyes closed and silently repeating a sound like "one" will do it, although this technique is perhaps better classified as a kind of meditation (see Chapter 9). "Autogenic training" is a well-researched procedure in which the subject is first trained to imagine the limbs becoming heavy and warm. Hypnosis generally involves entering a relaxed and receptive state of mind in which any suggestion by a therapist, or indeed one's suggestions to one-self, are more readily translated into physiological or behavioral change. Biofeedback uses information collected by machine, which is fed back to the subject, who can then shape his or her responses toward some desired result. When it is used to train people to relax, their muscle tension is monitored, and some indication of the level of tension is provided; for example, a tone may be emitted. As the subject relaxes, the pitch may go down, and so, by endeavoring to lower the tone further, the subject learns to make the kind of subtle internal adjustment that produces relaxation.

Deep relaxation is a skill to be learned, like riding a bicycle. It is not something that most of us can do without instruction and practice. After we have learned to achieve it in practice periods of perhaps twenty minutes once or twice daily, we can apply it to the rest of the day: the aim is to become aware of how our muscles are constantly tensing in response to thoughts and external situations, and to be as constantly "letting go" of this tension and not allowing it to build up into the kind of chronic, rigid patterns that cause headaches, back pain, general stiffness, and other discomfort. Awareness and control of how we breathe is an important part of this technique, slow, full breaths being associated with the relaxed state, and shallow, more rapid breathing with tension. We find that adjusting the body state toward relaxation concurrently affects our minds, making us more peaceful. It would be fair to say that relaxation is an essential prerequisite to many of the most important introspective methods, such as mental imaging, consulting an inner wisdom, and meditation, and to fuller awareness of our social and spiritual connections. When the body, and hence the mind, are tense and agitated, this seems to so preoccupy our attention that little else gets through.

Although relaxation is generally the most important skill to be learned at this level, a number of familiar areas of behavior affecting the body also usually need some adjustment to promote health. The importance of adequate rest hardly needs to be defended, and regular exercise, both aerobic and stretching, would also be understood by most people as an essential part of a healing journey. What to eat is a much more controversial subject. I have already pointed out (in Chapter 4) that there is no evidence that any of the unconventional diets or dietary additives have any effect on the course of existing cancer. The act of changing one's eating habits often has a powerful effect on a sense of control and optimism, however. At present, the best advice that can be given by therapists who are guided by available evidence, rather than by some preconceived or dogmatic view, is to eat a varied diet, including balanced contributions from the major food groups (fruits, vegetables, cereals, dairy products, some meat), keeping fats, salt, sugars, and such stimulants as caffeine and alcohol to a fairly low level.

## Conscious mind: level 2

The main aim at this level is to become aware of our thoughts, and to change them from their usual negative flavor into patterns of optimism and peace. Most of the time, we are not aware of what we are thinking, a fact that becomes obvious when we simply sit with our eyes closed and watch our minds for a few minutes. Yet this stream of unedited thoughts largely determines our mood and behavior. A common example is when a new, unfamiliar task is contemplated; we may feel incapable of doing it, and may think: "I've never been able to do that sort of thing, so if I tried I would fail and look ridiculous." As a result of such thinking, the challenge is avoided and some excuse is made—"There isn't time for that"—all without any awareness of what the underlying thoughts were. A feeling of depression and dissatisfaction may result from the unresolved conflict in a mind that simultaneously wants to act and is afraid to do so without realizing its ambivalence.

It is a fairly simple matter to become more aware, more often, of what we are thinking, to tap in to the stream, as it were. This is perhaps the central discipline in taking more control of one's life. We experience our thoughts as "who we are," as the core of our existence: they prompt our most visible behaviors, and as we learn to watch them more closely we find (as discussed above) that they affect our muscle tension and other less obvious bodily reactions to the world. Thoughts also determine mood. Many people constantly tell themselves, without being aware of doing so, that they are not good enough, or that things are too difficult or not how they should be, and these rather self-defeating ideas generate profound feelings of guilt, unworthiness, and depression. Cancer patients often create a stream of fearful thoughts about what might be in store for them. When they recognize that they are thinking this way, deliberate change is possible.

The relationship between thought and mood is now made use of in "cognitive" therapies, a variety of related techniques that have in common teaching people to recognize their negativity and substitute more realistic and mood-enhancing ideas. It is not so much that the thoughts themselves are *the* crucial determinant of our mood and behavior: in fact, all aspects or levels of ourselves are interconnected, as pointed out before, and changing any part will affect the whole. it is rather that thoughts are a very convenient and accessible place to make changes, with resulting effects throughout our being.

This is perhaps the place to say something about "positive thinking" or positive affirmations, a popular approach to self-change that has spawned quite an army of "therapists" who advocate simply believing and affirming what you want to see happen, in areas as diverse as physical healing and making money. Does this apparently simplistic technique work? We have very little in the way of objective data with which to assess it, but I think the answer is that it can have some effects, some of the time. Therapists with extensive training in more orthodox approaches usually decry such simple-minded maneuvers, pointing out, quite correctly in my view, that you can't just change mood by asserting that you feel great, without first acknowledging the self-denigrating and pessimistic thoughts lurking beneath the mental surface that created the mood. And, for physical healing, many determinants other than thought conspire to produce a given physiological state. Yet, the fact remains that vigorous, positive self-talk can have a remarkably beneficial effect on one's mood, at least in the short term, and I have met a number of cancer patients who swear by the process of never letting a pessimistic idea about their health cross their minds. We need research on the value of this attitude. Meanwhile, a prudent approach would be to experiment with affirmations for yourself, and if it feels comfortable, combine positive self-talk with an attempt to identify and discard any undermining negative ideas that you feel are unwarranted or unhelpful.

We could include the important business of having fun, or playing, in this section. A favorite cartoon of mine juxtaposes a group of children, happily playing, with a group of commuters, gloomily standing in a bus as they make their way to work. The caption is: "What happened?" The various pressures that stop us enjoying our lives are numerous and complex. By deliberately programming some enjoyable activities into our lives, even if doing so feels artificial or forced, we can greatly elevate our mood and so improve the quality of life. Even a diagnosis of cancer need not make us miserable if we are able to focus on the present rather than dreading the future. Perhaps, as Norman Cousins maintained, laughter can even heal or prolong life in some cases.[2]

## Deeper mind: level 3

The mind is a process, not a thing, in the same way that digestion is a process. Digestion depends on the functions of the gastrointestinal tract, which are relatively simple. Mind depends essentially on the function of the brain, which is incredibly complex—in fact, the most complex organized structure that we know of in the universe. The brain is made up of around a million million cells, many of them connected to one another, and from this sophisticated organic computer, many levels of function emerge. The most basic levels are concerned with regulating our internal organs, digestion, blood flow, breathing, and so on. The physiological states that underlie our emotions also arise from a fairly primitive part of our brain, and can be affected by the "higher" thinking functions, as we have seen. Our thinking powers are a recent evolutionary development; psychologists divide them into conscious processes, the stream of ideas into which we can tap at will, and relatively unconscious events, including fantasies, dreams, and ideas or memories that have been repressed (concealed) because they are painful to contemplate. The level of "deeper mind" is meant to include all of those processes, emotions, fantasies, and usually repressed material that can, however, be accessed when the conscious stream is quietened and attention is turned "within."

The two main topics to be covered in our early work on the deeper mind are emotional expression and the use of mental imagery as a healing tool. Experts argue about what emotions really are: for our purposes, they may be described as comprising a wide range of feelings, such as joy and sadness, anger and love, fear and fighting spirit. Emotions also play an important part in such complex human attitudes as hope, diffidence, ambivalence, embarrassment, and will to live. These are slippery things to define, yet they are immediately recognizable as part of our subjective experience. We would like to think of ourselves as rational creatures, guided by objective appraisals of situations; in fact we are largely driven by our emotions, often without being aware of it. Emotions can make us feel good, but also bring pain, and everyone learns to suppress (voluntarily) or repress (without being aware of it) some of life's most painful experiences and realizations. For example, the sense of helplessness that we often felt as children when confronted by a world of powerful adults is usually unrecognized when we attain adulthood ourselves, but nevertheless may remain within, dictating many of our activities. Some of us feel permanently helpless; others compensate by aggressive activity. A fortunate few had parents who made them feel loved unconditionally, and consequently are likely to be well adjusted as adults.

In the conflicting research on the "cancer personality," that is, attempts to define traits that are more common among cancer patients than among similar people without cancer, one feature stands out (as I mentioned in Chapter 5): cancer patients seem to have more trouble expressing emotion. As a consequence, it seems important for cancer patients to learn and practice emotional expression. How can we do this? By using the principles we have already discussed: first, becoming aware of the emotion whose expression is blocked, trying to pick up both the feelings in the body and the associated thoughts; then, deliberately expressing and discharging these ideas and feelings, either by talking frankly to others about them (usually the best way) or by at least acknowledging what the emotion is, and letting oneself experience it for a time. Other activities can help, such as exercise, prayer, relaxation, allowing oneself to cry, or shout, or sing, and even bashing a bed with a tennis racquet, if the emotion is intense anger. The principle is to let it out, let it "flow," although without imposing unduly on others. Emotions are sometimes described as "good" or "bad," meaning pleasant or painful, but it is more useful to see them as all part of life, and needing to be experienced and expressed. A relevant guiding phrase, often used by therapists, is: "The only bad emotion is a stuck emotion."

We turn now to the use of mental imaging in self-help, a topic important enough to need a section to itself.

## Mental imaging

The technique of mental imaging is the representation of aspects of our sensory experience in the mind. In other words, we imagine things when they are not actually present. Impressions of any of the senses may be represented internally in this way: we can evoke the smell of a rose just by thinking about it, the taste of honey, the touch of a cat's fur, or the sound of a distant bell. People vary in the kind of imagery that comes most easily to them, but for many visual imagery has most effect. All of us, with varying degrees of vividness, can conjure up pictures or impressions of the rooms we live in, the people we interact with, or scenes from a movie we saw last week.

Imagery is potentially important in healing because it may, in some circumstances, act as a blueprint or set of instructions to the body, as an intermediary between thoughts and physiological changes. This connection is most easily observed in situations where physical movement is contemplated; in such instances, if you watch your mind carefully, you will find that the decision to get up and go to another place, for example, is preceded by a transient image of the activity. Imagery also provokes more involuntary responses in the body: the effects of sexual imagery are familiar to all; fearful images can generate a stress response; the thought of sucking a lemon can promote salivation (try it!).

There are two main ways in which imagery might be useful for healing; we can call them the "diagnostic" and "therapeutic" modes. The diagnostic way of using mental imagery has a long history. It has probably been a part of many nontechnological cultures, and goes back in history at least to the use of healing dreams by the ancient Greeks and Egyptians. The central concept is that people can access, in their imagery, ideas or understandings not readily available to the rational mind. Since the time of Freud, we have recognized, in modern Western culture, that dreams may contain such hidden knowledge. Much of it may also be recovered in the relaxed waking state (as I will discuss in the next chapter).

The therapeutic use of mental imagery is an extension of the observation that images affect body function: it is argued by some that imagining beneficial changes, such as healing, may make it actually occur. Visualization of such healing changes was pioneered for cancer in the 1970s by Carl Simonton, a radiation oncologist, and Stephanie Mathews-Simonton, a psychotherapist. Their book (coauthored with J.L. Creighton) *Getting Well Again,* has been widely read by patients interested in helping themselves. The approach advocated in the book is to imagine and draw one's cancer, immune defenses, and medical treatment if any, endeavoring to see the disease as weak and the host resistance and treatment as strong and likely to overcome the disease. Images can be realistic pictures of cancer cells and immune cells, or symbolic figures, such as sharks eating small fish (cancer cells) or white knights spearing dragons. The approach is based on the Simontons' clinical experience, and on a study by their associates, Jeanne Achterberg and Frank Lawlis, who showed that there was a correlation between the optimism displayed in patients' imagery and their resistance to progress of the disease, at least in the short term.[3]

This technique makes a very strong claim: that you can directly influence the course of disease with your mind. It has had, and continues to have, a great deal of public appeal. It has been applied to many other diseases, and is frequently reported on by the media. In fact, it has become a rather standard mode of intervention for physical disease in the repertoire of many therapists teaching adjunctive self-help techniques. This is all the more remarkable because few orthodox physicians would attribute any power at all to mental imagery. What, then, should our assessment of this technique be?

You may recall from Chapter 4 that we can apply three criteria to new methods of treatment: is there evidence for its effectiveness, is there a consensus among knowledgeable people, and is there a rationale to explain how it might work? Looking first for evidence in the scientific and clinical literature, we find a number of anecdotal reports (descriptions of individual cases) where physical changes, such as cure of skin conditions, or immunological reactions, could reasonably be attributed to the use of imagery by the subject. Often, hypnosis was involved; that is, the patient imagined change while in a deeply relaxed state, susceptible to suggestion. However, I know of no scientific studies with adequate controls where mental imagery has been used as the sole or principal treatment mode to affect serious "organic" diseases like cancer. Also, equivocal results have been obtained in those few studies where attempts have been made to influence the immune system with imagery or suggestion in a group of subjects, and in which rigorous comparisons have been made to a control untreated group. This does not mean that imagery cannot affect immune function or disease progression, only that it is as yet unproven by conventional standards.

On the second criterion, consensus, we find an interesting situation in which many therapists are convinced of the value of mental imagery, whereas many other professionals reject it as quackery. I believe we should disregard those who denounce this approach without having made any study of the subject, and also those who make exaggerated, uncritical claims. This still leaves a large body of professionals who have found mental imagery very useful in their practices, ourselves included, and another group who feel there is no justification for believing that it can heal. I think most of us who employ the technique do so because it gives patients a sense of control, which is valuable in itself, and because we cherish the hope that there may well be healing effects, as yet undocumented. I would also add that, when my own cancer was active, I invoked images of large fish attacking it, and derived some reassurance from this: now that my disease is no longer active, I regularly use a nonaggressive, "balancing" kind of imagery, visualizing golden light filling each of my organ systems in turn. The rationale for a possible healing effect of imagery in cancer is that it is known to mediate many other kinds of changes in the body, as discussed above, and also to alleviate or heal a variety of less serious conditions in some people, such as pain, asthma, and some skin disorders. It thus seems not farfetched to propose that it might affect cancer, for example, by altering blood flow to tumors, or by changing levels of hormones in the body fluids, and making the internal environment less suitable for cancer growth. There must be severe restrictions on what imagery can do, however. If *any* suggestion could be translated into physical effects, the integrity of our bodies would be at risk (imagine if we were at the mercy of advice like "Drop dead!").

We badly need more research into the power of therapeutic imagery; at present, we have a situation in which large numbers of patients are reading about and trying the approach, the medical establishment is dismissing it, and money for research is very difficult to get because of the prevailing skepticism among those who dispense funds. There is no serious dispute among people who have worked with imagery about its abilities as an invaluable tool for diagnosing mental attitudes, a way of connecting with mental information and potential that might otherwise be inaccessible; we will return to this later. But its use as a healing agent is controversial; my own conclusion is that it certainly helps many cancer patients (and others) psychologically, and probably physically, but must be presented to them as an unproven remedy. It also should form only a part of a more comprehensive treatment plan.

## Social: level 4

Good communication is the key to having fulfilling relationships with other people. We must first listen to what others are saying, and let them know that we have heard. Then we need to express what we are thinking and feeling ourselves. This is perhaps very obvious, but it is frequently not achieved. The process of taking control at the social level is one of ensuring that we have good communication with those people in our lives who can support us, and that we avoid interactions that deplete our energies. We are supported when others listen empathically, affirm our essential worthwhileness, amuse, stimulate, and encourage us; we tend to feel "drained" when others satisfy their own needs at our expense, for example, by controlling or criticizing us.

For the person with a life-threatening disease, the most agonizing fear is often that of leaving loved ones behind. As one woman I knew put it, most poignantly: "I can't imagine a world without me in it!" Repairing and strengthening relationships with family members and important friends becomes a high priority for cancer patients who want to help themselves. This means taking time to be with these people, and taking the risk of telling them what they mean to you. We must reach out to people and "let them in." We may also need to drop long-standing resentments; forgive old hurts; and sometimes confront, asserting ourselves, where we may have avoided doing so, if we feel we have been unfairly treated. All of this is difficult, perhaps especially for most cancer patients, who may have difficulties with close relationships because they tend to repress their emotions.

Does such work on relationships promote healing? The recommendations made above are very general, and, if pursued, would help most of us, whether or not we have cancer, toward better social adjustment. It may be that there is great potential for healing in the social dimension; after all, many "primitive" cultures involve the whole group or community in elaborate healing rituals when one of their members gets sick. However, as is unfortunately often the case, we have little scientific evidence that better social connectedness favors healing. There is some experimental support for the idea that people who are more strongly connected to others are less at risk for a variety of diseases; we have already encountered the observation that men who have lost a spouse are more prone to cardiovascular disease than are still-married men. And in studies relating social support to cancer progression, most, but not all, have found a beneficial effect. Thus, in advocating that people work at improving their social relationships I am drawing mainly on clinical experience and popular wisdom; we are social beings, and nearly all people at least feel better when their social interactions are fulfilling.

This is perhaps an appropriate place to amplify what I said in Chapter 1 about the needs of family members and close friends of a cancer patient. The psychological suffering of a close family member or friend often seems to be as great or greater than that of the patient. The dominant fear is usually of losing a loved, supportive person, and wondering if life will be worthwhile or meaningful if they die. Clearly there is no simple antidote to this agony, but it can help to discuss and express love for each other. If we tell someone how much he or she means to us, before they die, at least we may later have the satisfaction of knowing that they understood this. Unfortunately, in the great need to deny the seriousness of the threat cancer poses, and in a society that avoids the topic of death, this kind of frank communication is often never achieved. People who are ill need to know that they are still worthwhile; in our punitive culture, there can be a stigma attached to being sick. They need the chance to fulfill as much of their normal role as health allows, and for optimal adjustment, to have people around them acknowledge the situation honestly, not covering it up with such remarks as: "You're gonna be all right," which, as I pointed out earlier, reflect the speakers' inability to cope.

Caregivers and family members have needs too. They may feel angry and resentful at the disruption to their lives and plans, and guilty about their inability to help. These emotions need to be expressed, preferably to someone other than the patient. And they continue to have a requirement for relaxation and diversion that is all the more important when they are looking after a sick relative. For health professionals who may make an emotional connection with hundreds of people who sicken and die over a few years, the risk is that they will become frustrated and "burnt out" at the disparity between what they would wish for these people and what actually happens to them. There is no simple remedy for this problem either, but, clearly, caregivers must pace themselves and attend to their own needs. It is also of help for caregivers to accept that they do not ultimately determine whether or not people get well, but can only do their best, and then accept whatever happens as part of some larger, unfolding plan.

### Spiritual (Existential): level 5

This very important and often neglected area of self-help is, unfortunately, not a level at which many people work in the early stages of their journey, unless they already have a strong spiritual or religious commitment. By "spiritual" I mean the sense of a universal order, plan, or intelligence, transcending individuals, and even the planet. It is to be distinguished from "religious," which refers to any system of faith or worship, not necessarily accompanied by spiritual experience.

We will postpone most of our discussion of spiritual aspects of healing to the next two chapters, in part because they are generally associated with more advanced work, and in part because the whole philosophy of "taking control" is antithetical to the spiritual search, which rather requires relinquishing it to a higher authority. Control must, however, be exerted over one's time and thoughts, in order to make a connection with the spiritual in ourselves. Doing so involves making time for such disciplines as meditation or prayer, for reading spiritual texts, and for attending functions like church services to experience the support of other interested people. Progress usually requires finding a suitable teacher, and orienting our lives away from self-satisfaction only and toward helping others.

## All levels together

For convenience, I have divided self-control procedures into five levels. A number of approaches clearly involve most or all of the levels at the same time. Stress management is one of these: in learning to notice and react less to stressors, we watch our bodies for signs of unnecessary reaction, monitor our thoughts and emotions, and pay particular attention to our social interactions as a potent source of disturbances to our equilibrium. We may also use spiritual practices to achieve calmness.

Another strategy that can't be easily assigned to any one level is goal-setting. The concept is a familiar one: we use our time in the best, most health-promoting manner possible if we have well-defined, fulfilling goals for our lives. It helps if these are stimulating, even exciting; we have all experienced the great emotional lift that often accompanies a new job or project or relationship. When we are ill we tend to tell ourselves: "Once I'm well again, I'll think about what I really want to do." In advocating goal-setting as a therapeutic process, I am suggesting that one should not wait, but instead clarify one's aspirations and work toward achieving them, on the grounds that this may assist healing. There is evidence that a state of mind labeled "hardiness," which involves approaching problems in a spirit of enjoying the challenge, taking control, and committing oneself to overcoming them, is associated with good health.

What our goals should be depends on the stage of disease, and must be decided by the individual. If someone is very ill, and likely to die within weeks or months, the most important tasks may be strengthening relationships, rather than beginning something new. If there is a fair chance of long-term survival, I encourage people to define and work toward things that they may have always wanted to do but have never seriously thought possible.

## Summary

In this chapter we have examined the rationale for the basic ways of "taking control," classifying the various approaches by the level of ourselves that is principally affected. At the body level, relaxation of muscular tension can be achieved by using well-studied techniques; this is seen as a prerequisite to most other self-help work. Attention to exercise, diet, and rest are also familiar ways of working at the body level to improve health. For the conscious mind, initially the main task is to become aware of the flow of thoughts, and to exert some control over what we tell ourselves. Under "deeper mind," we discussed emotional expression, and briefly evaluated the use of positive mental imaging, a technique that, although largely unproven, has become a very popular adjunctive therapy. The importance of developing good communication with others and warm, empathic relationships was seen as the main task at the social level. I briefly alluded to the spiritual level, deferring more detailed discussion until the next chapters.

# 9 Getting Connected

When we are faced with a crisis like cancer, our natural reaction is to try to reassert control, to bring our mental and physical life back to its previous state. In Chapter 8 we discussed the principles of rational self-control, including most of what is usually taught in hospital-based programs, as well as some techniques, such as mental imaging, that are not generally included in such programs. In this chapter, and the next, we venture into less conventional territory. We want to team how our various dimensions—physical, mental, social, spiritual—are related to one another, and to try to increase their interconnectedness. Control remains important, but is not the primary motive. Instead, the focus has shifted to *understanding*. As we move farther from orthodox technique, scientific proof of the healing power of increased connectedness becomes harder and harder to find, and we have to rely, instead, on the experiences of individuals, both patients and therapists, who have used the kinds of approaches we will describe. Much of what I cover in these chapters comes from the practice of different kinds of psychotherapy; some of it, particularly the spiritual viewpoint, derives from my own education, reading, and experience. I also touch on the frankly unorthodox area of paranormal experiences, which can lead us to a different view of reality.

## A restatement of the central concept

At this point, it is worth reiterating the basic viewpoint behind "connectedness" as the route to healing. This view holds that we are not separate from one another or from our world; that, instead, we represent localized concentrations of material and information, continuous with the rest of the universe. In Western culture, we tend to see ourselves as entities isolated from one another, from our environment, and even from our own bodies, which we often treat with scant respect. The reasons behind the closing off or separation are usually a misplaced fear of losing identity, of not getting what we want, and a consequent desire to control our surroundings as much as possible. In seeking "connectedness," we are aiming here at a world view more like that of certain other cultures, for example, the Navaho Indians, who see themselves and their land as part of an indivisible, intricate, and vital web. Despite Western cultural conditioning, we have a choice. We can close off our awareness from our surroundings, with the disastrous effects on the landscape that are now so obvious, or we can open ourselves to an awareness of interdependence with other living things. We can close ourselves off socially, or learn to empathize, and to experience love. We can ignore our own deeper minds and our spiritual being, or we can explore at least some of what is hidden, and begin to understand much more clearly who we really are.

Western medicine's view of healing is restricted to considering how external agents and procedures may change physical conditions in the body. It is concerned only with cause and effect, with a sequence of events in time. The connectedness viewpoint focuses much more on *relationships* than on events, with the way various parts of ourselves are related, and with the freedom of information (in the sense explained in Chapter 6) to flow from one part to another. My hypothesis is that strong relationships between our various dimensions will promote healing, by allowing the greater organizing power of the higher levels to balance out distortions in the lower levels. Thus, the nature of our work shifts, toward following the famous advice of Socrates: "Know thyself." It is really tragic how few of us take the chance to do so.

## Conscious mind: level 2

We will begin with the conscious mind, because it is primarily at this level that we adopt the habits that close us off from expanded potential. I make a strong claim here, endeavoring to justify it by rational argument, and finally describe the kinds of introspective approaches that will enable you to verify it for yourself. The claim is that we largely create our own "reality" with our minds. It is a view to which many psychotherapists and probably all mystics (spiritual seekers) would subscribe.

Although we are accustomed to thinking of the world as "given," exactly as we perceive it, philosophers from both East and West have long told us that we can't know what is really out there; all we know is the activity of our minds. The world must be very different to a dog, or to a bee: who is to say that the human species has the "real" perception? Closer to home, our cultural, racial, societal, and religious indoctrination determines much of what we take for granted: consider the kinds of sexual and racial discrimination that have been so common in many societies. An extreme case of the effects of environmental conditioning on our behavior comes from studies of rare instances of children who have been raised by wolves or other animals. In many ways, such a child is a wolf, in his or her reactions. Furthermore, within any one culture, each individual undergoes a unique set of learning experiences that determines how he or she views the world: if early treatment is harsh, for example, the world may become an unfair place, and other people will be seen as enemies to be fought against and exploited.

We thus have an elaborate series of filters—biological, psychological, cultural, and individual—that determine the characteristics of the world we think we perceive. Our thoughts and actions are driven by what we believe to be "out there," and we have to live in the limited world we create. Why does this matter? Apart from the fact that most of us would not choose to restrict our potential in this way, in the present context it matters because it greatly limits our ability to connect with all of ourselves, to get all of ourselves involved in healing, so to speak. Here are some examples of inhibitory attitudes that are very common among the cancer patients I have known: if we believe, as a result of early-life upbringing, that other people (parents) are criticizing us, we may grow up to see ourselves as basically guilty and unworthy. If we learn that emotional experience is best avoided, we may be inhibited from intimacy in relationships, and from making efforts to discover what we really feel about anything. If we have an exaggerated need to be in control of events, it will be extremely difficult to accept guidance by any "higher" authority, and hence to make spiritual progress.

How can we begin to liberate ourselves from our self-imposed prisons? Occasionally, under the stress of life-threatening disease, people make sudden leaps in their understanding, but, in general, it is a gradual, slow process. The central requirement is to *watch* the mind, to become an observer of one's own thinking. This learning is greatly helped by *writing down*, every day, what we have learned. A typical early experience might be: "I feel uncomfortable whenever I'm around him, but I'm not sure why. Perhaps he reminds me of somebody else. Come to think of it, he does act rather like my father used to—it's not that he looks the same, but his way of insisting on things is similar; it gets under my skin! But that's not fair; he's a different person from my father, and our relationship is entirely different. Next time we meet I'll try to be aware of what I'm thinking and not bring my childhood resentments into it." When the written record of such insights, in diary or journal form, is regularly reviewed, it becomes evident that we respond to different situations in a somewhat restricted number of ways. We come to recognize these patterns and catch ourselves repeating them, and so have some chance of breaking the cycle and making changes.

Whereas determined people can do a lot of this work by

themselves, perhaps in conjunction with reading about how the mind works (see "Further Reading"), it is extremely helpful, and probably essential, for most of us to have assistance from somebody trained in psychotherapy. This is so because we have all developed a number of psychological mechanisms, or "defenses," that we use to protect ourselves; the pattern and strength of these being different for each individual. They are often ineffective, or even harmful, and we are usually not aware that they are operating: nevertheless, we cling to them.

An example is the defense of projection: attributing to others impulses, such as hostility, that originate within ourselves. I remember a client who believed that almost everyone was out to take advantage of him: in fact, this perception was a reflection of his own attitude toward others. Another common example, as we have seen, is emotional repression: the seeds of this defense usually go back to early childhood, when we may have learned that our parents did not like us to express what we were feeling. To understand and alter these patterns, the serious student needs to find a helper who has had experience with how people's minds behave.

The variety of approaches to psychotherapy can be confusing when we begin to search for a therapist; I would advocate checking first that the person has been accredited by a recognized professional body, asking what experience he or she has had, and then attending a few trial sessions to see if you and the therapist can make a good connection. I cannot say that any one kind of therapy is better than others; you will need to look for a process and a person that challenge you but provide an environment of warm support. (On a personal note, after trying many kinds of psychotherapy in a half-hearted way, when I got cancer myself I began long-term, twice-weekly therapy with a good psychoanalytically trained psychiatrist, and found this extremely helpful, and complementary to my own efforts.)

Changing behaviors is not enough; we need to change our thoughts as well. This is not easy, and it must be acknowledged that not everyone seems capable of it. In particular, if we are sick, we simply may not have the energy and resolve to dismantle old patterns of thought or behavior, and in fact this should not be attempted if death is imminent. At such times, it is more important to strengthen our social and spiritual connectedness.

## Body: level 1

There is not much I can say in this section that goes beyond the obvious. Being more connected with our bodies involves becoming more aware of what they need, and supplying those needs. At the same time we will find that the mind often interferes by wanting things that the body does not need (an excess of tasty foods, for example). Much of our work at the body level is ultimately psychological: discriminating between true needs and the mind's desire for stimulation. We need to learn to view our bodies with affection, as trusty vehicles for our earthly experience, and as channels through which we can become more aware of material, psychological, and spiritual realities.

If we pay attention to the body's signals, we can sense what kinds of foods make us feel best: it is likely to be a lighter diet, as we progress, with less meat and fats. As we become more able to distinguish how the body feels when it is adequately rested and exercised, we will take the trouble to provide for these requirements. We all need to be touched by other human beings, and many have a strong urge for sexual expression. However, much of the "need" for sex, we may find, is imposed by the mind, which is assailed by sexual symbols through the media. Our sensitivity to the mind-body connection can be greatly increased by studying one of the body-awareness disciplines, such as the Indian technique of hatha yoga, a series of stretching postures with symbolic significance; or the Chinese t'ai chi, flowing body motions that have a meditative effect. I've had experience with both of these, and can vouch for their usefulness; however, you must find a good teacher. Other related techniques, developed in the West, are the Alexander and Feldenkreis methods, deep tissue massage, and Gendlin's "focusing," which is an attempt to make explicit the meaning of bodily sensations. If practiced diligently for a long time, most body-awareness techniques can yield "deep" (formerly unconscious) insights about the relationship of mind, body, and world.

As you explore the "bodywork" scene, you may find that, even more than in other areas of self-help instruction, the various approaches attract rather fanatical bands of devotees! Again, I can only suggest looking for credentials, examining the lives of the advocates and teachers themselves, to see if you admire what they have achieved, perhaps talking to their students, then trying a limited range of techniques, settling eventually on one method and sticking to it.

## Deeper mind: level 3

The "depth" metaphor is loosely used by mental health professionals to describe a range of functions of the mind. Some thoughts appear to be right "on the surface," as it were, and available to consciousness; we use these when we reason deliberately and self-consciously about events. Other thoughts are repressed, by the defense mechanisms we spoke of earlier; these are "deeper" in the sense of being more difficult to access. Then there are mental functions that seem to have evolved long before rational thought, such as emotions and, probably, imagery. And deeper still are automatic processes of the brain that control many activities within the body, such as heart rate, and are usually completely out of awareness, although we may influence them with higher processes, like imaging, or learn some control over them, for example, through biofeedback.

Since the deeper levels are closer to bodily functions, it is reasonable to suppose that getting in touch with them may be relevant to healing. The principal obstacle to doing so is our overdeveloped rationality. If we try to explore what we "really" feel about something, the conscious mind is likely to come up with a quick answer; for example, if we ask someone what it means to him or her to have cancer, the reply will usually be something conventional like "It scares me, because I might die and not be around to look after my family" (even the "scares me" part may take considerable questioning to elicit from some people!). But underneath this, that is, repressed and out of normal awareness, there may be other ideas and fantasies, which vary from one individual to another. In many instances, there may be a part of us that wants to die, perhaps because life is difficult and because death seems to be a way out, or a way for a normally "strong" person to attract sympathy and caring. Deeper feelings of profound guilt and unworthiness are not uncommon, cancer being seen as a justified punishment. If we are fully to come to grips with what our cancer means to us, we must be aware of these normally hidden ideas; if we do not, it will be very difficult to change them. The same, of course, applies to our true feelings about all aspects of our lives—for example, to how we view other people, or our job, or our marriage.

How are we to become more connected with our deeper minds? Traditionally, this task—of "making the unconscious conscious"— has been the aim of psychotherapy. Some kinds of therapy focus on childhood events and ideas, where most of our current patterns of thought originated; psychoanalysis is perhaps the most thoroughgoing method of this kind, requiring several sessions per week for a period of years. There is debate among professionals as to whether such intense examination of early life is necessary for change, and a number of briefer therapies have been developed that concentrate much more on the here and now. But whatever the method, any good psychotherapy makes us more aware of repressed ideas and emotions. We get a sense of what we "really" think and feel, of greater authenticity in our lives. We may not be more comfortable—in fact, particularly at first, psychotherapy may make us quite uncomfortable; for example, we may realize that our motives in many situations are self-serving, or that we feel anger toward someone we "should" love. However, these things have to be faced if we are to understand ourselves more fully, and thus have a firm basis for lasting change.

What can people do working alone? We can practice self-observation (described above) and we can learn to use mental imagery, in two ways: first, to find out what we deeply think and feel about something, and, second, to attempt to make changes in our attitudes or in our bodies, as we discussed in Chapter 8. For example, if, in a relaxed state, we imagine or picture somebody who is important to us, we may uncover previously unsuspected emotional reactions toward them beneath the smokescreen of superficial ideas that our conscious mind normally throws up. Then we can imagine forgiving them for hurt done to us, perhaps embracing or talking to them, or seeing them filled with light. Such exercises of the imagination can be applied to most aspects of life; we can use them to rehearse for feared events or to get what we want, often, it seems, with some effect. I would advocate that rather than simply trying to impose control over events, we connect first with what we think and feel at a deeper level—why we are afraid, why we hate someone, why we want to get well and whether there are some deeper reasons for "wanting" to remain ill. In this way, the approach described in this chapter differs from many of the "pop" methods of self-improvement that are now advertised.

Two further methods are well suited to individual efforts. Dreams tell us what is happening in the deeper mind, although, as Freud showed us, the messages they contain are often disguised. We all dream, and can learn to record and analyze our dreams (some instruction books are listed in "Further Reading"). The second mode of access to unconscious ideas is through meditation, which quietens the flow of conscious thoughts, making room, as it were, for other material to emerge; more about this later.

Here I want to introduce the very controversial subject of unorthodox or paranormal powers of the mind. Many people have experienced things that ought to be impossible according to our conventional ideas of space and time, for example, knowing what is in someone else's mind, even when that person is a long way away. We have to be careful that such experiences are not simply coincidences, but there have been controlled experiments that seem to show that, under some conditions, people can have an impression of what others are viewing several miles away. Then there is the phenomenon of precognition, or knowing in advance what is going to happen. I have had some completely convincing instances of this in my own life. This is perhaps a risky admission in that it may alienate readers who refuse to believe in such possibilities, but I feel that the only honest and truly scientific attitude is to be open-minded about the paranormal, while scrupulously looking for clues that we may be misleading ourselves.

A single dramatic, personal experience with such an event does tend to render irrelevant the arguments of those who hold them to be an illusion, much as the demonstration of flight by heavier-than-air machines refuted learned arguments, common before the Wright brothers, that aeroplanes were impossible. Another, even more bizarre kind of paranormal event is the "out of body" experience, where people see their bodies as if from a disembodied state, at a distance. I have known cancer patients who have had such experiences, both during relaxation exercises and while under anesthetic for surgery. "Near death" and "past life" incidents may be related to this. Accessing information from another sphere ("channeling") also contradicts our orthodox views.

Many people, when questioned, admit to having had such paranormal experiences; even after allowing for mistakes and deliberate deceptions, it appears that such experiences are not uncommon, and can be enhanced by training in mind-quietening techniques like meditation. This is not the place for a prolonged examination of their validity, but I have raised the issue here because of its possible relevance to healing. If precognition is possible, then the sequence of cause and effect in time is not unalterable: present actions might influence the past! And if we can have out-of-body experiences, this leads to the very comforting conclusion that we are more than just physical beings. Our five-ring map is inadequate, in that the deeper mind may merge with the spiritual. We will touch on this again in the next chapter, but should note here that modern physics is also telling us that our ideas of space and time are too limited; that time is not linear, but rather a construction of our own minds, and that particles like electrons may "know" what others are doing when widely separated.[1]

## Social: level 4

Better connection at the social level depends ultimately on better self-understanding at the psychological level. Our aim is to be able to drop grievances and instead feel love, express it (in our thoughts and actions, if not in so many words), and accept it from others. The principal blocks to this desirable state are that our own needs, fears, and sense of separateness are so strong that other people, with their correspondingly individual desires, inevitably frustrate us. By understanding these impulses, and working to override their dominance, we can greatly improve our relationships. Spiritual practices also help, by strengthening our feeling of unity with all things, as well as by quietening the clamor of sensory desires; meditators commonly report feelings of love toward others, even for people they don't know, and for animals and plants. But it has been my observation that spiritual practice alone will not do it for most of us: the psychological work is necessary. The social and the psychological levels, at this stage of our journey, are continuous, like the spiritual level and the deeper mind.

## Spiritual: level 5

The central spiritual idea is that we are all part of an order, power, or intelligence that is much greater than our individual selves. This order has been called by many names in different cultures: God, the "One," the Tao or Way, the Divine Order, Cosmic Intelligence. Sometimes it is treated as if it were a person: Allah, Yahweh, the Divine Father or Mother (since our first "gods" were our parents, it is natural for us to personify the power in this way). Historical individuals who had a strong spiritual connection are frequently considered gods or near-gods in themselves: Jesus, Buddha, and Ramakrishna, for example. Religions, which are codified systems of rituals and ideas, grow up around the spiritual experience of their founders, and of course vary greatly, but the underlying insights seem to be the same in different religions and cultures, and across the millennia. The spiritual part of our healing journey is learning to experience our place in this transcendent order.

How can we know that such an order exists? First, we have the similar testimony of the great mystics of many ages and cultures, remarkable people who have devoted their lives to understanding the spiritual. Most speak of "oneness," of universal love, of guidance available to the individual who seeks it. Then, if we are willing to consider it, there is the evidence of such paranormal events as "near-death experiences," in which people who have been close to dying often report passing through a tunnel, emerging into a region filled with love and light, perhaps seeing images of formerly deceased friends and relatives, only to be told that it is not yet their time and they must "go back"![2] These accounts might be dismissed as delirious, if it were not the case that so many of them are similar. But most convincing of all is personal knowledge, not the uncritical adoption of a comforting belief, but the actual experience of this transcendent order.

The skeptic may ask: "How is it that I haven't had such an experience?" An analogy may help. Imagine a person who has been walled up in a cave all of his life, and not told that other people exist, or told but unwilling to believe it. The social order would be largely inconceivable to such an individual; even if released, he would be unlikely to understand or relate to the community. Similarly, we all tend to be imprisoned by our thoughts, by our ingrained sense of separateness, and to deny what we can't see. Yet we have available the guidance of the great spiritual leaders of the world, and of many men and women throughout history who have made their own connection. An active role is required of the spiritual explorer; he or she needs open-mindedness and a willingness to follow some of the methods through which others have succeeded, but there is no need to accept any dogma uncritically; indeed, to do so may impede your own progress.

What are these methods? Some of the books listed in "Further Reading" discuss them, but the most important, according to my understanding, are as follows.

The mind needs to become *quiet,* for which purpose the various forms of meditation are designed. Meditation may be defined as awareness based on concentration in the relative absence of thought. It embraces a large body of techniques, all of which involve slowing down the normal stream of conscious thoughts, to produce an altered state of mind, which is like listening internally. Focusing on one idea, sound, symbol, or activity, and letting any other thoughts drop away, will produce such a state of relaxation and alert awareness. Some kinds of prayer may have a similar effect.

The deliberate cultivation, in one's life, of a sense of the sacredness of all things, and of humility, and gratitude and compassion for others, also helps to foster spiritual connection. Regular meetings with other people dedicated to the same search is probably essential for most of us. An orientation toward selfless service is important, as is a willingness to seek and accept guidance from this higher source. And along with these traditional spiritual approaches, it is important to do the psychological work of identifying and dropping the blocks to their implementation.

As with psychological insights, spiritual awareness may come suddenly (especially if life is threatened), but it usually grows gradually, over many years, when this kind of attitude to life is adopted. The egotistical self slowly diminishes in importance, and a sense of quiet joy and loving communion with others develops in its place. Awareness grows that death is not "the end," and, with this knowledge, the fear of death diminishes. (This pleasant state can, however, be easily shattered by stressful events, although it tends to return faster and persist longer with practice.)

These changes are desirable in themselves, and improve quality of life, but from the point of view of healing, the most relevant changes are perhaps the developing sense of meaning in all events (see Chapter 10) and the subjective experience of being loved and supported, a conviction that things will turn out well for us, even when we die. This feeling of being looked after, like other spiritual insights, is quite different from wishful thinking; it is, instead, a kind of inner "knowing," or intuition, that feels more reliable than thought. The materialist will shake his or her head at all of this, but it reflects both my own experience and that of many cancer patients I have talked to, particularly people who were dying. The reader should, however, realize that my descriptions of these states of consciousness are those of a relative beginner; for first-hand accounts of more advanced spiritual connectedness, the writings of the great mystics must be consulted (see "Further Reading").

## Summary

The search for connectedness goes beyond control to understanding what we think and do at all levels. The conscious mind is central to this process, and we must learn to do two main things with it: first, to observe our thoughts continuously, and, second, to stem this flow of thinking, at least occasionally. The observation of our thoughts, and the review of the written record of them, uncovers irrational, self-defeating, or depressive ideas and automatic patterns that direct our actions into unhealthy channels. Understanding deeper conflicts may require the help of a psychotherapist, although much can be done alone with mental imaging, meditation, and self-observation. With growing awareness, we are able to choose to give our body what it needs, and to drop some of the barriers to better interaction at the social level. The mental quietening not only relaxes us and makes room for repressed ideas to emerge but also allows awareness of the spiritual dimension, a self-transcending power, or order, to which we all belong. To strengthen our spiritual connectedness we can follow time-honored procedures: in addition to meditation, these include removing psychological obstacles and becoming actively receptive; cultivating such qualities as gratitude, humility, and compassion; reading spiritual texts; being of service to other people; meeting with like-minded others; and finding experienced teachers.

# 10 | Healing as a Search for Meaning

In this chapter, I attempt to gather together the strands from previous ones and offer a final, more global point of view—the broader perspective to which the search for healing from within finally leads us. We have seen that it is possible to become aware of previously unsuspected dimensions of ourselves, and consequently to exert more control over them. And we have examined some of the further benefits of pursuing this connectedness as an end in itself. A logical outgrowth of this journey is the awareness that everything that happens to us has "meaning" and fits into a larger scheme. This chapter attempts to explain rationally something that we eventually understand intuitively through the pursuit of self-understanding and connectedness: that diseases such as cancer may also be viewed as events with meaning. Healing from within is an active process, and may ultimately become a search for this meaning, in stark contrast to the orthodox conception of treating disease by external procedures, which might more accurately be called repair.

## A further extension of the connectedness model

Figure 11 shows the universe as a space-time continuum that appears to us to contain many separate objects or events (events are objects in motion). Physicists and philosophers tell us that every object is connected to every other: an event at one side of the globe creates a ripple effect that extends around the planet. Our idea of separateness is an illusion, as is our concept of linear time. However, we can choose to focus our attention on any part of the world we perceive, and I have shown a number of objects or events labeled 1 through 6 in the figure.

If we choose to view events as isolated from all others, then one of them, say number 2, will appear to be an "accident" with no cause or rationale. This view represents the most primitive state of knowledge, where observations are made but are not connected to other observations. It allows no prediction or control, and is thus liable to produce anxiety; magical explanations may be made to give the illusion of understanding, as in aboriginal cultures where, say, lightning is attributed to the anger of the gods. Our view of cancer has been not much more advanced than this for many years: it still tends to be regarded by many as a genetic accident.

The next stage in understanding is to try to connect an event to one or a few other dominant events, associated with the first in space or time. In the figure, we might examine numbers 1 and 3, to see if they are related to number 2. The result may be the development of "cause and effect" theories, if the events are closely connected. Such an analysis has worked quite well for infectious diseases, where contact with a micro-organism is a necessary condition for the infection to develop. It can never provide a complete understanding, however; for example, why do some people who are exposed to the micro-organism not get the disease? Other factors, such as a strong immune system, have to be investigated as well. And why does someone have a strong immunity? The search for final causes is never-ending. The simple cause-and-effect model has been applied to cancer at the genetic level, with the result that we now know that a series of mutations is necessary for a cell to

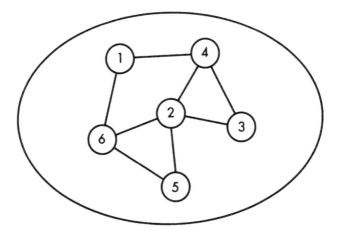

Figure 11

*The universe or cosmos appears to consist of many objects or events. All are interconnected, directly or indirectly; six of these events are shown. If number 2 represents getting cancer, it will seem like an accident if no connections to other events are recognized, or as having a "cause" if one or two dominant connections are identified. Cancer, or other disease, has "meaning" in relation to all other events in its vicinity, and ultimately in the cosmos.*

become cancerous (see Chapter 2). This is valuable knowledge, but it in no way constitutes a complete understanding, as it covers only a tiny fraction of the events that might be related to cancer; for example, we need to know why cancerous cells develop into clinical disease in some situations and not in others.

Finally, we can choose, at least in theory, to examine all other events in parallel with number 2, to determine what we might call "relationship" rather than cause and effect. There are obvious practical limits, but in our simplistic example this might mean looking at numbers 1 through 6. We can also choose our level of analysis: in the case of cancer, we might consider molecular, cellular, organ level, psychological, social, or spiritual ones. The higher levels involve clustering a number of factors together, not worrying about the fine detail; so, in our simplistic example, a social analysis of contributors to cancer might be equivalent to examining the impact of two composite elements, (1+3) and (4+5+6). As we have also seen, we can choose to pay attention mainly to mass/energy interactions, which is more usual, or to focus on informational or pattern events, which we are beginning to recognize as a valuable kind of analysis; the psychological, for example, is a purely informational concept.

I hope it will be clear that I am not saying that cause-and-effect analysis is wrong and the relationship approach correct: the former is simply a much more restricted way of fitting an event into a context of other events, to be used whenever it works; the latter is an idealized way of trying to encompass all events, including local causes, that might affect the one in which we are interested. If the universe of relationships is an orange, the cause-and-effect model is a slice through part of it. Our criteria have to be pragmatic: we use any way of understanding events that allows us to predict and control them, the simpler the model the better. What is unjustified is to rule out certain connections without examining them, as the psychological level has often been dismissed in cancer. It is the relative failure of materialistic, causal analysis of cancer that makes it necessary to use a broader approach.

## Does cancer have meaning?

"Meaning" is a difficult word. What does it signify? When we ask of any event whether it has meaning we usually intend to enquire why it happened, what it was designed to accomplish, or how it fits into a broader pattern of events. For example, a car accident might be understood purely as chance collision of vehicles, or as a result of impaired driving by one of the people involved, which, in turn, might be attributed to alcohol abuse brought on by stressful social conditions, and so on. The net of connections is potentially endless, but we will feel our understanding of the event to be more and more secure as we know more about all related factors. The meaning of the event is its *relationship* to other events, how it fits into the web of associated happenings.

Cancer is also an event or process, albeit a slow-motion one. It, too, must have meaning in this sense; that is, it is inextricably related to many other events in the patient, in his or her environment, and in the world. The meaning of cancer, according to this view, derives from these relationships. All events have such meaning; life has meaning. If we deny meaning to cancer, we are denying it to our lives, and to everything else.

"Meaning" is often understood in more restricted ways than the one I am using here. The word is still used as a synonym for cause or consequence, or to denote the way we perceive something in our minds. Thus, a disease might "mean" that our lives are at risk. Psychoanalysts speak of certain diseases, including cancer (in the opinion of some), as being projections of mental conflicts into the body; breast cancer has been attributed to an expression of frustrated nurturing needs, for example. These ideas are hard to prove, and represent a much more limited application of the term "meaning." To other people, cancer is seen as a "lesson" or even a punishment for imagined misdeeds; this quasi-spiritual (and sometimes harmful) view attempts to understand one's misfortune in relation to presumed laws of nature or of some higher being.

The advantage of the very broad "connectedness" view or model of cancer and other events is that it allows us to consider them in relationship to any other events at any level we choose. It makes no prejudgments as to what is possible, and asks only what descriptions are useful. The meaning of cancer is its relationship to these other events. Thus, we are free to operate at only the biological level if we wish, to understand the disease and its treatment as exclusively biological processes. At the other end of the spectrum, we are also free to ask about the spiritual implications of getting cancer, and how we might work spiritually to help ourselves against it. The same applies to social and psychological levels of meaning.

We can see now that it makes equally good sense to use "top-down" or "bottom-up" therapy; that is, to work at the higher or lower levels. These approaches are complementary, not contradictory. The model of the human being as hierarchical levels of organization linked to everything else provides a rationale for healing strategies that have been known intuitively and used for millennia in many cultures. We choose to employ the massive, local, material alterations that characterize modern medical treatment, but we also begin to understand the much more diffuse, all encompassing, symbolic (informational) changes that are indicated by the connectedness viewpoint. The test of the value of this broad theoretical approach will come from experiments based on it, but we need the theory to conceive of the experiments we might do!

The searches for understanding and for healing are thus closely similar. We understand something when we perceive its relationship to other events; the more connections we can make, the "deeper" our understanding feels, and the stronger our sense of the meaning of the event becomes. Healing, likewise, derives from strengthening connections, in order not only to understand with our rational minds but to experience with our whole being our relatedness to all other things.

## Writing one's life story

In practical terms, how can we work at uncovering meaning in our lives and disease? Almost any activity, including one's normal daily round, can be a path to an understanding of meaning, if done with awareness and concentration. In our own courses for cancer patients, we focus on three principal methods. The first is writing a life story or autobiography, which reveals meaning, particularly at the level of conscious mind and social interactions. The second is hard to label, but involves trying to get in touch with inner sources of unconscious wisdom through such techniques as watching dreams and holding "dialogues" with an "Inner Healer," revealing meaning mainly at the level of body and deeper mind. The third is the spiritual search.

The aim of the life story is to examine all aspects of our lives, and write about them. Usually, the student has never attempted this before, and the exercise proves to be very exciting and rewarding. It can be done in many ways, but we suggest looking at the following twelve areas: (1) current events or status in our lives, (2) the major "stepping stones" or branching points in our lives, (3) family history, (4) education, (5) career or life work, (6) major crises, (7) health, (8) sex, (9) interests and hobbies, (10) relationships, (11) experiences of death, and (12) development of meaning and values. In addition to simple reflection and recalling of past events, we can also use imaging and meditation; recording of relevant dreams; talking with family members and friends; and making up "collages" using old photos, mementos, and any other important objects. We can try to have a dialogue with our "inner child," or attempt to define different "subpersonalities" that may be active at various times—for example, "career person," "wife/husband," "parent," "fighter," or "wimp." We can write letters (without sending them) to people from our past. When we are finished, we could relate the "story" to a sympathetic listener or group.

As we go through this exercise, patterns of behavior and thinking emerge that were often unsuspected. We may see, for example, that we have tended to avoid challenges, or, conversely, that we were risk-takers in many situations. We may come to understand that early choices, or an early image of ourselves ("I'm no good at...") can profoundly influence the course of later life. We may learn why we have done whatever we have. When the story is completed, our cancer will be seen against the backdrop of a much richer picture of who we are.

Constructing this detailed description of our lives is of great value in itself. If the patient is dying, it can provide some "closure" or sense of completion. But it also may suggest what are the most fulfilling and life-affirming paths for us to follow from this time on, and may point to important roads as yet untraveled. Several experienced therapists have emphasized how vital it is to discover and pursue whatever we are "meant to do" in our lives. Lawrence LeShan writes of the central importance of learning to "sing our own song";[1] W. Brugh Joy says, "The soul must learn to find its own way."[2] There are many anecdotes, although no hard evidence, of cancer patients being helped by clarifying what is truly important to them, and changing their lives to pursue it. Writing a life story, together with keeping a diary and, if possible, engaging in ongoing psychotherapy, may thus provide a strong sense of meaning or purpose in life. In combination with spiritual work (described below), it may also enable us eventually to forgive other people for any perceived harm done to us, and allow the development of a degree of unconditional love for others and fuller acceptance of our present situation.

It is evident, as LeShan emphasizes, that just wanting to return to or maintain exactly the same life situation that existed before cancer is unlikely to promote healing, although it is a common and culturally sanctioned aspiration. If, for example, we have a primary tumor removed but we fail to change, residual cancer cells will find their environment essentially the same as the one they had grown in before: this environment may allow further growth. Only if we *change* this environment, by changing our patterns of thought and behavior, can we expect these cancer cells to be inhibited from multiplying further. I know I have said this before, but I repeat it here, because I have been saddened by watching hundreds of people go through an operation for removal of a primary cancer, then refuse to acknowledge the seriousness of what has happened to them, and simply return to "business as usual."

## Getting in touch with inner knowledge

A great deal of evidence exists that the deeper or unconscious mind has both a detailed knowledge or record of events in the body and much potential to control them. We can learn both to "tap into" this potential to some extent, and to exert some conscious influence, in a number of ways. For example, our dreams may graphically reveal unsuspected thoughts and feelings about our cancer, its treatment, or other related aspects of life. I vividly remember a dream I had a few days before my colon surgery that showed the surgeon as a house painter, going to the trouble of removing a length of piping in order to paint thoroughly under a join: this seemed to indicate my confidence in him. It is quite simple to learn to analyze your dreams (some instructional books are listed in "Further Reading"), and you may find this a rich source of information about your "deeper" feelings.

Some control can be exercised more directly over many body functions that were formerly thought of as automatic through biofeedback, hypnosis, and the use of mental imaging, as was discussed earlier. In these instances, a subtle awareness of internal cues develops, allowing control. Some remarkable individuals have even been able voluntarily to stop blood flow from large wounds, or to tolerate abdominal surgery without anesthetic. This demonstrates potential that presumably lies in us all but is developed in very few. You may come across the idea that symptoms in the body are an expression of mental conflict; that, for example, asthma is a "suppressed cry of help for the mother," or that breast cancer represents some kind of ambivalence about nurturing. This kind of thinking was popular among psychoanalysts at one time, although it seems to have rather gone out of fashion. However, it has been embraced by some New Age health writers: you can find lists of diseases with their psychological "meanings" neatly attached in certain of these books. What are we to make of this? We can see from our own experiences that there is some relationship between mental events and bodily reactions when we observe our responses to stress, as discussed in Chapter 8: for example, patterns of muscular tension, like the hunched shoulders that go with fear or the stiffness in any set of muscles that are ready to act but are held back. There is, however, very little direct evidence for the view that a disease like cancer is "psychosomatic," that is, a mental conflict played out in the body. Some responsible professional therapists claim that a deeply buried conflict, such as memory of sexual abuse in childhood, may underlie some cancers, and that bringing this to light may assist cure, but this is very much a minority, unproven view. However, in terms of the broader theory we have been discussing, it is evident that all symptoms involve all levels of the individual, and thus must have physical and mental dimensions; those distinguished as "psychosomatic" are simply cases where the psychological involvement is more obvious.

On a more practical note, we can begin our search for the meaning of our cancer, its relationship to other parts of our life, by using mental imagery in a relaxed state. A widely used technique is to take an imaginary trip inside the body to "visit" a source of inner wisdom, usually imagined as a wise person or spiritual figure. A "dialogue" may then be entered into, along the lines of greeting this figure and asking "What should I do to help myself?" In our experience, people who are open-minded enough to use this technique may derive great reassurance and help from it, although the "answers" tend to be general in nature.

A related technique, involving the diagnostic use of mental

imaging that was mentioned in Chapter 8, is to "visit" one's cancer in the imagination, trying to determine what it "looks like" to the inner eye—its size and shape, feel, color, texture, and any other qualities that come to mind. At the end of the exercise, the patient may draw the cancer, his or her immune defenses, any treatment, the whole body, and other aspects of life that seem relevant. The diagrams can tell the patient a great deal about how he or she is reacting emotionally to the cancer, and how it is seen in relation to life as a whole. A skilled interpreter is usually needed, however; this technique is, in fact, a kind of art therapy and is quite widely used in psychology, although not commonly applied to physical disease. According to some therapists, it may also be possible to get a sense of what the cancer "wants" through imagery (that is, what needs it is fulfilling), although I have found that people tend to fabricate answers to this question. If there is a real wish-fulfillment or mental conflict represented in the cancer, it is very difficult to access authentically.

These are ways to try to find meaning in disease—how it relates to other events in ourselves, over and above the purely biological connections. Our understanding of and research into these approaches are embryonic as yet. People who work with such techniques a lot are often convinced of their great potential, but because of our limited knowledge, and because of the great resistance many individuals have to exploring such methods thoroughly, it is only the occasional "remarkable" patient who exhibits physical change as a result.

### Spiritual search

As we move from the center outwards on our diagram of the person (see Figure 5, page 90), we pass through levels that are increasingly larger and more complex: they contain more and more information, in the sense we discussed earlier. Thus, we might expect that they become increasingly powerful, in the same way that there is increasing power as we ascend the levels of a large manufacturing organization, from the factory floor, through middle management, to the chief executive's office. The "lower" levels can, of course, shut down the whole operation, much as a few aberrant cells in our body can sabotage our health, but, in general, it is the highest levels that have the power to make the most far-reaching changes. I have represented the spiritual dimension as corresponding to the structure of the universe as a whole. If this is so, it is reasonable to propose that the spiritual level has ultimately the greatest power to heal. The problem is getting in touch with it effectively; we tend, instead, to identify with the individual factory hand.

In Chapter 9, I listed some of the traditional ways people have tried to become more aware of their intrinsic spiritual potential, to connect with their spiritual level. It is a long, hard struggle for most of us, a journey that we never complete in life, because we cling to our imagined separateness so strongly. Yet the aim of the spiritual search is clear: it is to see everything, every event, not just as material, psychological, or social, but as spiritual, as something that has meaning against a broad canvas transcending space and time. We have to align ourselves with, or attune to, an order much greater than ourselves. Even a little progress on this path brings great benefits that we have already alluded to: some mental peace, a feeling of being supported, a realization that death is not the end.

Can spiritual connectedness bring healing? There are many who have claimed so. It is difficult to investigate scientifically, both because such connectedness is hard to assess in a valid way, and because few people change much over a short time. I've described our beginning attempts to relate psychological and spiritual change to healing in Chapter 5; these results fit with my clinical impression that when people make strong progress spiritually there is a good chance of some physical healing, as well as healing in the sense of increased connectedness at all other levels. However, I do not think that the relationship between spiritual awareness and physical health is simple. We do not see the whole picture. Death may seem to us agonizingly premature, yet it may not be without reason.

Sometimes I am asked, particularly by scientific colleagues, how there can be any role for the spiritual, or even the psychological, when cancer can be explained "completely" as a genetic change. Another way of putting essentially the same question is to ask why animals get cancer, when their minds and spirits are presumably not developed, the suggestion being that material explanations alone must suffice. To understand the answer to this question, we need to look again at Figure 5. Every event occurs at all levels: cancer is simultaneously a biochemical, genetic, cellular, and social event. It is also a psychological and spiritual event to the extent that these levels are developed; when they are not, the disease remains a more purely biological phenomenon. We humans have a unique opportunity to find meaning at these higher levels and to use them in the service of healing.

"What meaning can I hope to find in my own disease if I explore the spiritual level?" This is the practical question, the point everyone comes to when he or she undertakes a serious healing journey. There can be no general answer; each of us must make his or her own investigation. I can tell you my own experience so far. At age forty-seven, I was diagnosed as having a serious bowel carcinoma that had spread to some of the local lymph nodes. After surgery and some chemotherapy, my chances of long-term survival were said to be about one in three. While convalescing, I went to a center for spiritual studies and did an intensive three-month course aimed at understanding myself better at the psychological and spiritual levels. This exposure, as well as my prior spiritual work and my subsequent increased efforts, has made it quite clear to me that there is a larger purpose. I have had a number of clear "spiritual" experiences, and some that were paranormal. Several "recurrence" false alarms have also kept me working! I discovered a part of myself that would as soon die (to avoid the effort that I associate with living) and have had to acknowledge this, and come to terms with it. What the purpose of the rest of my life is I don't pretend to know exactly, but I am clear that my task is to maintain a connection to the higher order and to respond to the guidance that is always available. This comes whenever I am mentally quiet and receptive, not so much in words (although there have been one or two startling verbal "communications"), but as "knowing" or feeling what to do. The main obstacle is my self-centeredness: constantly wanting to do things for my own gratification or to fulfill an imagined need for self-protection.

This story, with variations, could be repeated by many people who have survived a crisis. It is not particularly dramatic, and it is not certain that my own efforts have made any physical difference, but what is clear is that my willingness to search for meaning in events has lifted my view of the world to a different, and broader, level. I still see things as biological, but also as psychological and spiritual. There is a strong sense of symbolic meaning in every-thing that happens, of rich interconnectedness between all events.

Many people have reached this point in their understanding, and some have gone much further; I have sought out such people to learn more. The disease may come back, and threaten to kill me; if it does, I will try to "fight" it, in the sense of mustering my courage to face it squarely, and will continue to strive for an under-standing of what it has to teach me, and ultimately for acceptance of death, when it comes. This is what I would wish for all people with life-threatening disease, and it is the attitude I have observed in and learned from those of our patients who have progressed most in their healing journeys.

## Summary

In this chapter, I put forward the view that the "meaning" of an event lies in its relationship to other events; this concept is broader than cause and effect, which refers to a simple linear chain of occurrences. Cancer, like any other phenomenon, has meaning, in the sense that it has a relationship to many other events, both within the body and outside it. The search for meaning in cancer, or in any event, is the attempt to place it in its physical, psycholog-ical, social, and spiritual context; growing understanding may or may not be accompanied by physical healing, but will bring com-fort, an awareness of our connectedness, a lessened fear of death, and a sense of authenticity and purpose in life. We briefly looked at three specific approaches: writing a life story; dialoguing with an inner source of unconscious wisdom, personified as an "Inner Healer"; and further efforts to connect spiritually.

# 11 | Summary: The Healing Response to Crisis

We have arrived, in a roundabout way, at a point of view that many reach intuitively: events in our lives, including life-threatening illness, are not accidents but are connected to everything else that happens to us at physical, psychological, social, and spiritual levels. This relationship or connectedness confers meaning on illness; exploring this meaning helps us to respond in an authentic, human way to the crisis and may promote physical healing. This is not a conclusion that can be backed up with much scientific evidence as yet; a scientist might prefer to call it a hypothesis. It is, however, an understanding that many people—cancer patients and others—have gained through their own efforts to know themselves and to make sense of the problems they encounter. I hope that intuitive readers will forgive my belaboring of what may be obvious to them, and will understand that I am trying to ground their insights in logical thinking and available evidence. I am aware, however, that what has been presented here is not enough to convince many biomedically oriented professionals; such a challenge will have to await a much longer and more technical study.

We looked first at what cancer is, and noted that the disease is caused by the body's failure to control the proliferation of genetically altered cells; we discovered that it is logical to use therapies that may strengthen this control, including psychological interventions that may have effects on immune, hormonal, and nervous systems. We drew a distinction between treatment from outside, which includes medical intervention and many unorthodox remedies, and healing from within, by which is meant the effects of any consciously initiated patterns of thought, emotion, and behavior.

In our discussion of external treatments, we noted that medical procedures are often curative for early-stage cancers, but seldom more than palliative for advanced disease. We then looked at ways of evaluating unorthodox "external" remedies, which are usually dietary or "immune" in nature, and concluded that there is no evidence that any are effective. While making no strong claims for the general effectiveness of healing from within, we briefly reviewed evidence suggesting that the mind does have an effect on the development and progression of cancer, and thus provides a relevant avenue for adjunctive treatment of the disease.

In the second half of the book a theory was developed to explain how the body, mind, social, and spiritual levels might interact. It was suggested that health is promoted by the optimal flow of information between all parts and levels of a person. The strategy of self-initiated healing depends on increasing the connectedness of all of these parts and levels. Three main stages in this self-help work were identified: taking control, getting connected, and searching for meaning. Together, they make up a progressive healing journey. Many different techniques may be used on this journey, but the most important endeavors are to become aware of our flow of thoughts and feelings, of at least some of our unconscious ideas, and of our relationship to a transcendent spiritual order.

Our view of cancer and other crises can be different from the usual popular conception. Of course, it is a fearful, agonizing discovery to learn that one has cancer. However, cancer is not an "evil" thing, but part of life's experiences, and may be accepted as an inducement to get on with the central task of understanding who we are. I have known many people who responded in this way, and

I have tried to do so myself. We are not so much looking for a "key" to cancer cure as using cancer as the key to self-discovery. Physical healing may follow—one hopes so, although evidence is scant as yet—but it becomes a byproduct of the search. The ultimate tragedy is not to die, but to die without making the most of our opportunities for personal understanding.

This attitude to life and crisis is not at all new, just something that is being rediscovered in the field of health. Why is it still so foreign to our health care system in the West? Some of the reasons have to do with patients, and some with health professionals and the system within which they operate. For people with severe illness, it is easier to deny the seriousness of the situation and leave the care of the problem to others who are perceived as powerful. When we are hurt, we retreat and just want a "quick fix," or for somebody to make things better. This is an immature, although understandable response, one that would not be respected in other areas of life where initiative is applauded. A passive reaction to chronic health problems is, however, tacitly encouraged by many health professionals, whose skepticism about the ability of people to help themselves is often based on a lack of knowledge of the possibilities or a wish to retain control over patients' health care. Such communications as "There's nothing you can do; go home and try not to think about it," while well meant, may gravely undermine a person's spirit. Admittedly, it is difficult to help people change, but, in the long run, it is much more rewarding than treating them as helpless. There is an urgent need for those of us within the health care system to inform ourselves and our patients about what it is possible for them to do to help themselves. If we dismiss contemptuously the impact of psychological, social, and spiritual realms on healing, we are no better than the "New Age missionaries" whose pronouncements we are quick to deplore.

How can an open-minded person make his or her own evaluation of healing from within? The obvious way to begin, as in most fields, is by reading widely. I have listed some starting material in "Further Reading." The scientifically minded can consult the literature on mind-body interactions. As well, there are a large number of "popular" books, which vary greatly in quality; some are patently biased and unfounded; others are the stories of individuals who have struggled honestly with crises in a way that commands respect. Still others have been written by people trained in the sciences, who have expanded their horizons by introspective practice: the present book is one of these. Sooner or later, however, the sincere student of healing from within must begin his or her personal exploration, within the terrain of his or her own mind. We can read all we want about psychological dynamics, but we will not believe the extent to which people are propelled by unconscious ideas until we discover it in our own lives. The influence of mind on body also needs to be explored within ourselves, and the spiritual search can be conducted only in the quiet space where thinking stops.

The role of the health professional, whatever his or her primary discipline, can be something much more than mere repair. He or she can be a teacher, a guide in the discovery of meaning in illness and in life. This is not a grandiose view: a teacher is simply a fellow-traveler with a few more years of experience than the student. It is not required that the teacher has been ill, but it is necessary, if he or she is to function in this role, that he or she be engaged sincerely in seeking personal meaning. There is, I believe, a widespread hunger for this approach to healing, but it is obscured by the stultifying materialism of our culture, the consequent mechanical nature of most standard treatments for disease, and the prevailing lack of appreciation for the power of our higher dimensions.

If you are a cancer patient, my appeal to you is to aim higher than simply having someone else take your disease away, so that you can forget all about it; use the experience to learn about yourself, and do whatever you can to contribute to your healing. It may or may not make a visible difference to the disease, but you will derive great satisfaction from the attempt. If you are a health professional working with cancer patients, my hope is that you will train yourself not only in the conventional rational scientific way of attempting to alleviate disease but also in the intuitive approach of personal knowledge. I have tried to bridge these two cultures in this book. It will not convince everyone. I hope it proves a useful synthesis for some.

# Notes

These notes make reference mainly to specific technical material or to one of a few, key "popular" texts. For more general background reading, consult "Further Reading."

CHAPTER 2

1. J. Laszlo, *Understanding Cancer* (New York: Harper and Row, 1987).

CHAPTER 4

1. B.R. Cassileth and H. Brown, "Unorthodox cancer medicine," *CA—A Cancer Journal for Clinicians* 38(1988): 176–86.

2. B.R. Cassileth, E.J. Lusk, T.B. Strouse, and B.J. Bodenheimer, "Contemporary unorthodox treatments in cancer medicine," *Annals of Internal Medicine* 101(1984): 105–12.

3. T. Kaptchuk and M. Croucher, *The Healing Arts* (New York: Summit Books, 1987).

4. E. Ernst and B.R. Cassileth, "The prevalence of complementary/alternative medicine in cancer," *Cancer* 83(1998): 777–782.

5. S. Barrett and V. Herbert, "Questionable cancer remedies," in: J. Holland et al., eds.: *Cancer Medicine ($4^{th}$ edition)*, New York, Williams and Wilkins, pp. 1459–1467.

6. S. Clinton and E. Giovanucci, "Nutrition in the etiology and prevention of cancer," in: J. Holland et al, eds.: *Cancer Medicine ($4^{th}$ edition)*, New York, Williams and Wilkins, pp. 465–494.

7. M. Lerner, *Choices in Healing* (Cambridge, Mass.: MIT Press, 1994).

CHAPTER 5
1. L. Sklar and H. Anisman, "Stress and cancer," *Psychological Bulletin* 89(1981): 369–406.
2. B. Klopfer, "Psychological variables in human cancer," *Journal of Projective Techniques* 21(1957): 331–40.
3. D. Spiegel, J.R. Bloom, H.C. Kraemer, and E. Gottheil, "Effect of psychosocial treatment on survival of patients with metastatic breast cancer," *Lancet*, Oct. 14, 1989, 888–91.
4. A.J. Cunningham, C.V.I. Edmonds, G.P. Jenkins, H. Pollack, G.A. Lockwood, and D. Warr, "A randomized controlled trial of the effects of group psychological therapy on survival in women with metastatic breast cancer," *Psychooncology* 7(1998): 508–517.
5. L. LeShan, *Cancer as a Turning Point* (New York: E.P. Dutton, 1989).
6. O.C. Simonton, S. Mathews-Simonton, and J.L. Creighton, *Getting Well Again* (New York: Bantam, 1980).

CHAPTER 6
1. G. Engel, "The need for a new medical model: a challenge for biomedicine," *Science* 196(1977): 129–36.
2. L. LeShan, *Cancer as a Turning Point* (New York: E.P. Dutton, 1989).
3. A.M. De la Pena, *The Psychobiology of Cancer: Automatization and Boredom in Health and Disease* (New York: J.F. Bergin, 1983).
4. J. Campbell, *The Hero with a Thousand Faces* (Princeton, N.J.: Princeton University Press, 1972).

CHAPTER 7
1. V. Frankl, *Man's Search for Meaning* (New York: Simon and Schuster, 1959).
2. B.R. Cassileth, E.J. Lusk, T.B. Strouse, and B.J. Bodenheimer, "Contemporary unorthodox treatments in cancer medicine," *Annals of Internal Medicine* 101(1984): 105–12.

CHAPTER 8
1. H. Benson, *The Relaxation Response* (New York: William Morrow, 1975).
2. N. Cousins, *Anatomy of an Illness as Perceived by the Patient* (New York: W.W. Norton, 1980).
3. J. Achterberg and G.F. Lawlis, *Imagery of Cancer* (Chicago: Institute for Personality and Ability Testing, 1978).

CHAPTER 9
1. F. Capra, *The Tao of Physics* (New York: Bantam, 1975).
2. R. Moody, *Life After Life* (New York: Bantam, 1975).

CHAPTER 10
1. L. LeShan, *Cancer as a Turning Point* (New York: E.P. Dutton, 1989).
2. W. Brugh Joy, *Joy's Way* (Los Angeles: J.P. Tarcher, 1979).

# Further Reading

Listed here are some popular (i.e., nontechnical) books relevant to the healing influence of mind and spirit.

GENERAL CANCER SELF-HELP

Allen, J.E. *The Five Stages of Getting Well.* Portland, Oregon: Life Time Publishing, 1992. An excellent account of the changes needed for healing.

Clyne, Rachael. *Coping with Cancer.* New York: Thorson's Publishing, 1986. An overview of self-help methods.

Cunningham, A.J. *Helping Yourself.* Toronto: Canadian Cancer Society, 1989. A workbook and two audiotapes, which can be obtained from the Canadian Cancer Society, 10 Alcorn St., Suite 200, Toronto M4V 3B1.

Dass, R., and Gorman, P. *How Can I Help?* New York: Knopf, 1986. A truly beautiful book for the person who wants to help others.

Dosdall, Claude. *My God I Thought You'd Died.* Toronto: Seal Books, 1986. A cancer survivor's inspiring account of his quest for health.

Epstein, A.H. *Mind, Fantasy and Healing.* New York, Delacorte Press, 1989. A fascinating account of the dedicated use of imagery for healing.

Gawler, I. *You Can Conquer Cancer.* Melbourne: Hill of Content Pub., 1984. A cancer survivor describes the many things he did to assist his recovery.

Hirshberg, C. and Barasch, M.I. *Remarkable Recovery.* New York: Riverhead Books, 1995. Stories of remarkable healing.

Jevne, R.F. and Levitan, A. *No Time for Nonsense—Self Help for the Seriously Ill.* San Diego: LuraMedia, 1989. Pragmatic and good-humored view of self-help strategies.

Lerner, Michael. *Choices in Healing.* Cambridge, Massachusetts: The MIT Press, 1994. An excellent and comprehensive description of alternative therapies for cancer patients.

LeShan, L. *Cancer as a Turning Point.* New York: E.P. Dutton, 1989. A recent statement of LeShan's views on self-healing.

————. *You Can Fight for Your Life.* New York: Jove/HBJ, 1977. Psychological self-help for cancer, by a pioneer researcher in this field.

Mathews-Simonton, S. *The Healing Family.* New York: Bantam Books, 1984. An excellent book for families supporting a cancer patient.

Morra, M. and Potts, E. *Choices.* New York: Avon Books, 1987. A complete handbook on possibilities in cancer treatment.

Pennington, S. *Healing Yourself.* Toronto: McGraw-Hill Ryerson, 1988. An inspiring account of qualitative research with six cancer patients who greatly outlived their life expectancies.

Shinoda Bolen, J. *Close to the Bone.* New York: Touchstone, 1996. A Jungian analyst looks at life-threatening illness and the search for meaning.

Siegel, B. *Love, Medicine and Miracles.* San Francisco: Harper & Row, 1986. Best-selling account by a surgeon who advocates psychological self-help.

Simon, D. *Return to Wholeness.* New York: John Wiley & Sons, 1999. Mind, body and spirit approaches to fighting cancer.

Simonton, O.C., S. Mathews-Simonton, and J.L. Creighton. *Getting Well Again.* New York: Bantam Books, 1978. A very well-known early guide emphasizing imaging.

Spiegel, D. *Living Beyond Limits.* New York: Time Books, Random House, 1993. Description of how group psychotherapy helped women with metastatic breast cancer live longer.

Wilbur, K. T. and Wilbur, K. *Grace and Grit: Spirituality and Healing in the Life and Death of Treya Killam Wilbur.* Boston: Shamblala, 1993. A moving personal story of healing.

**OTHER PSYCHOLOGICAL SELF-HELP BOOKS**

Achterberg, J. *Imagery in Healing: Shamanism and Modern Medicine.* Boston: Shambhala, 1985. One of several fine books by Dr. Achterberg on the subject of imagery.

Barasch, M.I. *The Healing Path.* New York: Penguin Books, 1993. On mind-body healing.

Benson, H. *The Relaxation Response.* New York: William Morrow, 1975. On the value and practice of relaxation—a classic.

Benson, H. and Stark, M. *Timeless Healing: The Power and Biology of Belief.* New York: Scribner, 1996. A successor to Benson's classic "Relaxation Response."

Bertherat, T. and Bernstein, C. *The Body Has Its Reasons.* Avon Books, 1976. A simple book on body awareness.

Borysenko, J. *Guilt is the Teacher. Love is the Lesson.* New York: Warner Books, 1990. Very readable account by a modern teacher.

Borysenko, J. *Minding the Body, Mending the Mind.* New York: Addison-Wesley, 1987. An excellent account of self-help ideas.

Bresler, D. *Free Yourself From Pain.* Simon and Schuster, 1979. Discusses many of the imagery and self-examination methods.

Burns, D. *Feeling Good: The New Mood Therapy.* Hearst, 1992. An excellent guide to thought changing.

Cameron, Julia. *The Artist's Way.* New York: Tarcher/Putnam, 1992. A course in discovering and recovering your creative self.

Carlson, R. and Shield, B., eds. *Healers on Healing.* Los Angeles: Jeremy P. Tarcher, 1989.

Davis, M., Eshelman, E.R. and McKay, M. *The Relaxation and Stress Reduction Workbook.* California: New Harbinger Publications, 1982. A manual for self practice.

Epstein, G. *Healing Visualizations.* New York: Bantam New Age, 1989. Specific suggestions for imagery and pointers for getting started.

Fanning, P. *Visualization for Change.* Oakland Calif.: New Harbinger Publications, 1988.

Faraday, A. *Dream Power.* New York: Berkley Medallion Books, 1972. A study of dream analysis.

Garfield, P. *Creative Dreaming.* New York: Ballantine Books, 1974. A study of dream analysis.

Gendlin, E.T. *Focusing.* New York: Bantam Books, 1980. Exploring the mind's ability to "listen to" the body.

Jampolsky, G.G. *Love Is Letting Go of Fear.* New York: Bantam Books, 1979. Very simple and nice; Jampolsky's other books are also highly recommended.

Kabat-Zinn, J. *Full Catastrophe Living.* New York: Delacorte Press, 1990. An excellent, comprehensive account of the use of awareness and meditation for healing.

Kaptchuk, T. and Croucher, M. *The Healing Arts.* New York: Summit Books, 1987.

Kripalu Centre. *The Self-Health Guide.* New York: Kripalu Publications USA, 1980. An excellent self-help book based on principles of yoga.

LeCron, L. *Self Hypnotism.* Englewood Cliffs, N.J.: Prentice-Hall, 1964. The basics of self-hypnosis.

Levine, Stephen. *A Year to Live. How to Live This Year As If It Were Your Last.* New York: Bell Tower, 1997. Exactly as it says; doing the exercise.

Levine, S. *Healing into Life and Death.* Garden City, New York: Anchor Press, Doubleday, 1987. Levine's books bear the stamp of his own profound development.

Lewis, L.C. *Be Restored to Health.* Best Sellers, 1982. Excellent "how-to" book on self-help and lifestyle.

Locke, S., and Colligan, D. *The Healer Within.* New York: E.P. Dutton, 1986. Scientific background for healing from within, written in a very accessible style.

Ornish, Dean. *Love & Survival.* The Scientific Basis for the Healing Power of Intimacy. New York: Harper Collins, 1997. A very readable account of the impact of love on health.

Pelletier, K. *Mind as Healer, Mind as Slayer.* New York: Delta, 1977. Mainly about stress, and the effects of mind on body.

Rossman, M.L. *Healing Yourself.* New York: Pocket Books, 1987. An excellent, professional guide to mental imagery.

Ryan, R.S. and Travis, J.W. *Wellness Workbook.* Berkeley: Ten Speed Press, 1981. A comprehensive manual on how you can work toward wellness at all levels.

Samuels, M. *Healing with the Mind's Eye.* New York: Summit Books, 1990. On mental imagery.

Samuels, M. and Samuels, N. *Seeing with the Mind's Eye.* New York: Random House, 1975. On visualization.

Weil, A. *Spontaneous Healing.* New York: Knopf, 1995. Recent account of mind-body healing by a physician.

## MEDITATION AND SPIRITUAL MATTERS

*A Course in Miracles,* Foundation for Inner Peace, and Viking Books, 1975,1996. A truly remarkable book for the dedicated seeker. Includes daily lessons to deepen spiritual awareness.

Bedard, J. *Lotus in the Fire, The Healing Power of Zen.* Boston: Shambhala, 1999. A down-to-earth personal account of how the teachings of Zen helped one man survive terminal illness.

Bodian, S., ed. *Meditation for Dummies.* Forest City: IDG Books Worldwide, 1999. A comprehensive guide to meditation.

Boorstein, S. *That's Funny, You don't look Buddhist.* New York: Harper Collins, 1997. How you can be both an observant Jew and a passionately committed Buddhist.

Dass, R. *Journey of Awakening: A Meditator's Guidebook.* New York: Bantam, 1978. A very helpful book by an American teacher.

Dossey, L. *Healing Words: The Power of Prayer and the Practice of Medicine.* San Francisco: Harper, 1993. A comprehensive book by a physician on the relationship between prayer and healing.

Easwaran, E. *Meditation.* Petaluma, Calif.: Nilgiri Press, 1978. Simple and excellent.

Easwaran, E. *The Undiscovered Country: Exploring the Promise of Death.* Tomales, Nilgiri Press, 1996. A spiritual approach to learning more from death; like all of Easwaran's books, beautifully written and highly accessible.

Frankl, V. *Man's Search for Meaning.* New York: Simon and Schuster, 1959. A famous but simple book, relating meaning in life to survival and health.

Gawler, Ian. *Peace of Mind.* Bridgeport, Dorset: Prism Press, 1987.

Gawler, I. *Meditation. Pure and Simple.* Melbourne: Hill of Content, 1996. A simple and excellent guide on meditation.

Hanh, T.N. *The Miracle of Mindfulness.* Boston: Beacon Press, 1976. A simple book on self-awareness by a Buddhist master.

Harpur, T. *The Uncommon Touch.* Toronto: McClelland & Stewart, 1994. Christian account of healing.

Kabat-Zinn, J. *Full Catastrophe Living.* New York: Delacorte Press, 1990. A comprehensive account of the use of awareness and meditation for healing.

Kabat-Zinn, J. *Wherever You Go, There You Are.* New York: Hyperion, 1994. A very popular follow-up to *Full Catastrophe Living.*

Kornfield, J. *A Path with Heart*. New York: Bantam Books, 1993. A book on the spiritual journey by a well-known Buddhist thinker and writer.

Kushner, H.S. *When Bad Things Happen to Good People*. New York: Schocken Books, 1981. A comforting book that helps you search for meaning in having a disease.

LeShan, L. *How to Meditate*. New York: Bantam Books, 1974. Practical advice and psychological ideas.

Levine, S. *Who Dies?* New York: Anchor Books, 1982. Raising our awareness about life and death; all of Levine's books are valuable.

Moody, R.A. *Life After Life*. New York: Bantam Books, 1975. Case histories of people who had near-death experiences, suggesting that there is "life after death."

Radha, Swami S. *Mantras, Words of Power*. Kootenay Bay: Timeless Books, 1980. The use of mantra for meditation, by a present-day spiritual master; all of Swami Radha's books are valuable.

Underhill, E. *Practical Mysticism*. London: P.J.M. Dent, 1914; Harmondsworth, Middlesex: Penguin Books, 1970. A classic, very readable book on the spiritual path.

Watts, A. *Meditation*. Several paperback editions. Watts has written many books interpreting Eastern spiritual ideas for Westerners.

Wilbur, K. *No Boundary*. Boulder and London: Shambhala, 1981. A very clear exposition of the connectedness of all things.

Yogananda, P. *Autobiography of a Yogi*. Self Realization Fellowship. Twelfth edition, 1993. A classical work; an account of the development of a spiritual master. Very readable.

# Index